Bridging the Gaps

Contextualization among Korean Nazarene Churches in America

In-Gyeong Kim Lundell

Originally published by Peter Lang Publishing, Inc., 1995

ISBN-13 978-1-945975-57-8
ISBN-10 1945975571

Reprint Published by EA Books, Inc.
eabooksonline.com

DEDICATION

To

every Korean and American Nazarene pastor

who struggles for the Kingdom of God,

especially to those who work hand in hand

ACKNOWLEDGMENTS

I am deeply indebted to all those who supported and prayed for me over almost a decade of seminary education. I am indebted to all the then parishioners of L.A. Korean Nazarene Mission Church (now Praise Church), Calvary Korean Church, KAMSA Church, and Agape Family who understood and tolerated me while I was researching and writing. My deep appreciation goes to pastoral colleagues of the L.A. District Church of the Nazarene, who accepted and encouraged me to work together in their church buildings and to then L.A. District Superintendent Dr. Paul Benefiel, who understood and supported me through many struggles in my personal ministry while I was preparing this study.

I am grateful to the professors of Bethany Nazarene College (now Southern Nazarene University) for their teaching and encouragement. I am deeply grateful for the contributions and teaching of many professors in the Schools of Theology and World Missions at Fuller Theological Seminary, under whom I had the privilege of studying. My deep appreciation goes to Dr. Dean Gilliland, who advised the writing of this manuscript.

I am most grateful to Dr. and Mrs. Chan Woo Huh and Mrs. So Ja Lee, who faithfully prayed for and supported my study and ministry, then to my praying and loving parents, brother and sisters, and to my children, Daniel, John and Grace, who stood with me through many years of studies.

My inexpressible debt of love is to my husband, Peter Lundell. Without his insightful criticism, and long, patient editing, this book may have remained forever incomplete.

CONTENTS

FOREWORD by Dean S. Gilliland

1 INTRODUCTION 1

    Why Contextualization
    Why I Write
    Problems We Face

2 THE RISE OF THE CHURCH OF THE NAZARENE
   U.S.A. 11

    The Holiness Movement: History of Formation
    The Form and Plan of Organization
    Church Doctrine and Government

3 CONTEXTUALIZATION 26

    General Overview
    The Need for Contextualization
    Models of Contextualization
    Criteria for Contextualization
    Characteristics of Contextualization

4 KOREAN WORLDVIEW (A): SHAMANISM 46

    General Worldview Theory
    Functions of Worldview
    Korean Worldview
    Summary

5 KOREAN WORLDVIEW (B): BUDDHISM,
   CONFUCIANISM AND CHRISTIANITY 69

    The Buddhistic Dimension
    The Confucian Dimension
    The Christian Dimension

6 COMPARISON OF KOREAN AND AMERICAN
WORLDVIEW

    THEMES..850

        Space and Time

        Causality

        Self and Others

        Relationship

        Acculturation

7 THE KOREAN CHURCH OF THE NAZARENE IN THE
U.S.A. 117

        Immigration

        A Brief History of the Korean Church of the Nazarene in
        Southern California

        Problems Faced By The Korean Nazarene Church

        General and Special Rules of the Church of the Nazarene
        Constitution

        Theological Issues

        Leadership Issues

8 CONTEXTUALIZATION AND CONCLUSION:
TOWARD DOING A THEOLOGY FOR KOREAN
NAZARENES IN SOUTHERN CALIFORNIA 139

        A New Perspective

        Contents and Containers

        The Trajectory Principle

        Contextualizing Cultural Issues

        Contextualizing Theological Issues

        General Rules and Cultural Appropriateness

        Conversion

        Contextualizing Ecclesiological Issues

IN PARTING..167

NOTES 169

REFERENCES CITED 172

FOREWORD

Imagine what might have happened in apostolic times if Jerusalem Christians had been allowed to govern the churches in Antioch, Galatia or as far as Rome. To begin with new expressions in the Holy Spirit may never have been released; worship would have been imprisoned in Jewish forms, and powerful questions of truth arising from non-Jewish believers would never have penetrated the thick walls of tradition. But what would have been the saddest and most hopeless of outcomes? It is this. We could not even speak of a church among the gentiles. Non-Jews would never have been attracted to the gospel. The body of Christ would have been little more than a ghetto-ized enclave of Jerusalem believers, honoring themselves for "keeping the faith" and judging all others by their own history. That would have spelled the death of the church.

But God intervened in ways that changed the witness of the church for all time. God provided missionary situations that forced the Jerusalem church to face the need for changes, to bend hallowed rules and introduce innovations so that the saving work of Jesus Christ could become good news for *all* people, gentiles as well as Jews. No, it was not an easy time for those early Christians. The record of confrontations, controversy and compromise is clear enough in the Acts of the Apostles and the letters of Paul. But giving up precious practices and agreeing to changes is why the apostolic churches survived and became such dynamic mission centers.

I have a special relationship to Rev. Dr. Kim Lundell, because when she took my class called Doing Theology in Context a fire was started in her head and heart. While she continued to minister and study a conviction grew within her. She felt that her Church had failed to see how long-standing Nazarene convictions and the deepest needs of Korean people were in conflict. Dr. Lundell is convicted of this New Testament principle, namely, the Word must become flesh and be made to dwell among real people, that Jesus must be born into each human situation as truly as He was born in Jerusalem. The gospel must take root and thrive in every human culture just as it grew among the Jews in Palestine during Jesus' time.

A statement that Dr. Lundell makes at the very beginning of her book shows the problem she faced as a Korean pastor working in the American Nazarene Church. These are her own words: "As a coordinator of the Los Angeles District, I have had long experience in church planting among Korean immigrants in the Nazarene setting. Yet our church planting and growth (among Koreans) appears to be an almost impossible mission."

Facing this problem head on, while maintaining a love and loyalty for her Church, is what lies behind everything she writes.

To accomplish this the author took on a task, which called for several components. She begins by setting out the kinds of problems that arise from historic Nazarene convictions. The question is since conversion, holiness, lifestyle, and church governance are so critical to Nazarenes, why have these not transferred well to Korean Christians? To understand this dilemma her book takes up Nazarene history with special emphasis on holiness theology and standards for the spiritual life held by the Church. This last point is important in that the Nazarene Church is a product of a special time and place, namely the U.S.A., with roots in the nineteenth century. This leads her to show what is meant by the term contextualization. Contextualization seeks to establish the absolute essentials of the biblical gospel and to separate these from cultural elements that become associated with the gospel but are not of its essence.

Dr. Lundell next introduces the reader to the way in which the Korean person views his/her world of reality. This is information that the Church leadership needs if the Word maintains high hopes for Korean Nazarenes, because Koreans have welcomed the news of Jesus Christ as a great people group. Everything Kim Lundell writes is done from her years of ministry, which have been undergirded by the practice of spiritual gifts. She does not write to show off her academic ability but to share her own insights as an insider both to her people and her denomination. God bless you as you read these pages, and may our Lord Jesus be honored with new growth and spiritual power in the Church.

Dean S. Gilliland
Professor of Contextual Theology
School of World Mission
Fuller Theological Seminary

Chapter 1

Introduction

Several years of cross-cultural ministry left me frustrated and discouraged. In 1983 I planted a church and was pastor of a very new congregation in Los Angeles, California. During that time I encountered numerous problems with denominational district activities, policies, rules and regulations due to cultural and linguistic barriers.

I found the cultural and linguistic differences between the American Church of the Nazarene and the Korean Church of the Nazarene produced problems in receiving members, establishing lay leaders and bringing immigrants into the church. As Eugene Nida observed, "Cultural differences are ever-present barriers to communication" (1954:221). Only a few American pastors were trained in or sensitive to cross-cultural ministries.

Koreans were from a monolithic content of one culture, one language and one tradition. An unbridgeable gap stood between their native context and the host American context. I found how important it was to understand the differing contexts in order to communicate the gospel and nurture a church. This led me to ask if efforts at contextualization might hold out some hope.

Why Contextualization?

Some actual examples may help clarify the problem. In 1985 my brother took over my pastorate in Los Angeles. The situation

1

became unfavorable because of the difficult relationships between the American and Korean congregations. I was acting as a coordinator of the L.A. District and was caught in the middle.

In 1986 I endeavored to plant another congregation near Garden Grove, but the local pastor discouraged my ministry by limiting use of the building to only two hours on Sunday. I gave up. Later I tried to start another congregation in Northridge for six months but encountered similar restrictions. Another Korean pastor, Jae Don Yang, tried to plant a Korean congregation in the North Hollywood Church of the Nazarene but was told to leave the church due to culturally related conflicts between the two congregations. Other problems occurred because of such things as the noise of unsupervised children.

It became apparent to me that Korean congregations were not appreciated in the Nazarene structure, because of their seemingly uncooperative attitude and their lack of participation in local or district level activities. This was due to cultural, linguistic and worldview differences which underlay all areas of their social interaction.

These kinds of problems are not found among Korean churches situated in Korea. They occur when Koreans are under American church leadership and do not know how to speak, think or act as Americans do.

Anglo Americans are the dominant group and, therefore, expect Koreans to accept their value system and social norms as well as adopt similar behavior patterns, both in the communication of the gospel and in operation of the church.

First generation Korean immigrants face many problems in family and society as well as in their emotional and psychological, behavior. One third of my students live under stepparents in broken family situations; this would be very unlikely in Korea. Koreans designated as "1.5-generation Koreans" are those who came to America in their childhood or teens and grew up here. They are more bicultural and bilingual than the second generation. They struggle to adapt and adjust to American culture, schooling, social life, and status quo.

Second generation Koreans are born and raised in America and are called American by birth. But in cultural identity they are neither Americans nor Koreans. Second generation Koreans have conflicts with the Korean culture, yet they belong to the Korean community.

The following is a commercial illustration of conceptualization. When I came to California in 1982 I stepped into an Alpha Beta Market for grocery shopping on Olympic Boulevard and Catalina Avenue in Koreatown. I was astonished to see all the traditional and authentic Korean food on the shelves, including the smelly *kimchi* and fermented fish. Of course almost all of the shoppers were Koreans. I felt as if I were in an open market in Korea.

Outwardly, it was certainly an American grocery store, but its food was for Koreans, since the owners knew their clientele. The groceries had to be presented in a way in which Koreans would buy and eat. Eventually, the store was purchased by Koreans.

This is the rationale of contextualization, to open a spiritual food store and present the products in a way that is attractive and relevant to Korean taste, so that Koreans might buy and eat and receive eternal life. This, I believe, was the way of Jesus.

I propose taking context into consideration for the sake of relevant gospel communication to first- and 1.5-generation Koreans in the U.S.A., particularly southern California. The study is divided into three parts: preliminary considerations, practical considerations, and application.

This first chapter introduces the study and presents the contextual problems of the Korean Church of the Nazarene in the U.S.A. Chapter 2 deals historically with the beginnings of the American Church of the Nazarene in order to study the roots of its context and its development of church government and theology. Chapter 3 surveys contextualization through its brief history, theory, and areas of needs, models, and criteria.

Chapter 4 deals with worldview theory within an historical and anthropological context and with the shamanistic dimension of Korean worldview Chapter 5 continues to discuss Korean worldview regarding Buddhistic, Confucian, and Christian dimension. Chapter 6 looks at the differences between Korean and American worldview themes accounting for the conflicts between Korean immigrants and the American Church of the Nazarene. Chapter 7 discusses the Korean Church of the Nazarene with respect to its history of growth and problems encountered in the specific area of theology as they related to conversion, people movements, meaning of holiness, and leadership training.

The final chapter presents a trajectory principle of conceptualization as a way of doing theology in the Korean immigrant context and recommends ways in which the American Church can help meet the cultural, theological and ecclesiological needs of Korean Christians.

Why I Write

The fact that there is such a small number of Korean Churches of the Nazarene presents a limitation. As a Korean woman I have frequently encountered the frustrations of cultural boundaries. Being a first generation Korean immigrant myself, I still find myself having difficulties in grasping American worldview and culture.

I am focusing my study on Korean immigrant churches within the Church of the Nazarene among the first and 1.5-generation Koreans.

Anthropological and social insights will be applied primarily to worldview and acculturation. I will limit the area of my conceptualization to theology and ecclesiology. Churches in Southern California will provide the cases observed.

While studying at Bethany Nazarene College in Oklahoma City, I worked for the Korean Church of the Nazarene, where I could observe the problems. While studying at Fuller Theological Seminary, I worked for two different Korean churches, observing and identifying additional problems. I observed and counseled numerous pastors whose church planting attempts failed. Thereafter, I made several efforts to plant new congregations in Koreatown L.A., Orange County, San Gabriel Valley, and San Fernando Valley. The result of this was that only two churches were actually planted while the other attempts were unsuccessful.

I have observed problems of the Korean Church of the Nazarene by doing ministry in the field and by consulting with other pastors who work with the American pastors in the L.A. area or other major cities in the U.S.A. I have lived with them and tasted that failure, and still I am encountering those problems in my ministries with the 1.5 generation.

My purpose is to discover ways to bridge cultural gaps between mainstream American culture and first and 1.5-generation Koreans in America in order to build the church in ways relevant to their cultural and linguistic context.

The observations I intend to make will apply to the Church of the Nazarene in its outreach to Korean immigrants. Since new Korean Nazarene churches are generally housed within American church facilities and are under the jurisdiction of American District Superintendents, the problems of cultural differences and linguistic barriers are obvious. This study pursues possible solutions in dealing with these issues.

Therefore, I will explore the roots of the American Church of the Nazarene, which itself is a particular contextualization of both theology and church. The prototype of the Church of the Nazarene originated in a particular American cultural context at the turn of the century. Holiness theology, which had already been developed, was rethought and advocated in new ways within the historical Wesleyan traditions.

The American Church is the seedbed for the Church of the Nazarene as a denomination, which is deeply anchored in American worldview and is a product of American history. Naturally, re-contextualization is called for if non-American congregations are to survive. Thus, my research will examine and compare American worldview themes to Korean worldview themes so that we might discern ways to present the gospel relevantly to Korean immigrants in the church of the Nazarene.

In particular, the theologies of conversion, the Holy Spirit and ecclesiology need to be contextualized for better communication of Christian Truth for Koreans. Therefore, it is significant to study the differences between worldviews in order to understand cultural systems through which the gospel is communicated.

As a Korean coordinator of the Los Angeles District, I have had long experience in church planting among Korean immigrants in the Nazarene setting. Yet our church planting and growth appear to be an almost impossible mission.

This study seeks to call attention of cross-cultural workers to theologize seriously by considering anthropological perspectives and worldview themes in both cultures. The largest Korean population outside of Korea is in California. If the Church of the

Nazarene intends to expand Korean ministries, this is the region where it must happen. But Koreans living in California are different from those in Korea. Thus this study pleads for the doing of theology in context, whether by Koreans or by American Churches of the Nazarene.

It is imperative to remember that a culture and its worldview are the very core of the context. Paul Hiebert articulated the problem clearly when he said, "Differences in world view are the most difficult of all cultural differences to bridge" (quoted in Charles Kraft 1982:10.2). This study insists that evangelization and church planting must begin with a consideration of issues on the worldview level. It neither seeks to present a finished theology nor to involve the whole of anthropology, but rather attempts to show how the degree of understanding worldview can affect the success or failure of churches.

Problems We Face

The contextual problem we are dealing with is multifaceted.

Theological problems can be identified in the areas of conversion and holiness; problems arise in the areas of ecclesiology and use of worship facilities; and immigrant families themselves face problems of identity.

Each problem must be understood as part of the whole, and the problem as a whole stands between, and is defined by, two very different cultural backgrounds.

The Problem of a Theology of Conversion

In 1984 as a single woman pastor of a new congregation, I encountered a disturbing situation. I was faced with accepting new members who could not quit drinking or smoking. There were two men who became Christians and had made very dramatic changes in their lives, turning away from old relationships, beliefs and ways. Yet they had not completely changed.

In a pastoral staff meeting I talked about receiving these new converts into membership in the Church of the Nazarene but was turned down and told to wait until they quit smoking. Therefore, I went to my District Superintendent hoping to solve the problem of receiving them as members.

The District Superintendent brought the *Manual of the Church of the Nazarene* and I brought the Bible for a lengthy discussion of the situation.

The conclusion was that according to the *Manual* they had to stay on probational membership. My heart was sad because I knew that they were changing and wanted to be members of the church. Being part of a group oriented culture they must have felt unaccepted and ashamed. I wanted to tell the District Superintendent that these new converts were different from those fully accepted Nazarene members who didn't smoke or drink but were, nevertheless, nominal Christians. These new converts would grow and eventually quit the old habits, but to do so the church needed to enfold them and nurture them as family members.

This negative encounter with the hierarchy of the Church was the first stimulant toward my study of contextualization. I believe the nature of the problem lies in the differences of worldviews, cultural contexts and in a theology of conversion.

The major question here is: Is conversion a completed, static state, or is it a point of entry? While the American Church of the Nazarene has roots in American worldview and culture, Koreans have their own roots in Shamanism and Confucianism. Each worldview is integrated into cultural social subsystems and will influence our answers.

The Problem of a Theology of Holiness

Entire sanctification is the distinctive doctrine of the Church of the Nazarene. But this presents problems for Koreans due to certain prohibitions put on holiness by the Nazarene Church that do not correspond with the understanding of "holiness" in the Korean situation.

Having a strong sense of the sacred and profane and coming out of a polydemonic, animistic, Buddhistic-Confucian background, Koreans are, in general, actually more open to the concept of holiness than Westerners.

Therefore, the definition and power of holiness needs to be expounded in terms that Koreans understand. Because of the profound differences of worldview between Koreans and Americans, the forms and meanings of holiness can be very dissimilar.

7

Koreans seek the *power* of holiness as more important than the *scruples* or rules of lifestyle that Westerners expect. Coming out of a demonic kind of background, Koreans view mental or physical Illness differently from Westerners who have a more scientific worldview. If the traditional shaman heals the sick and exorcises demons, a pastor can hardly direct his parishioners to hospitals or mental institutions and expect to be an effective leader. Entire sanctification thus needs to be understood not only as a holy life but also as a triumphant life.

The Problem of Ecclesiology

It was not easy for me to pioneer and pastor a congregation as a Korean woman. First, the Church of the Nazarene is not well known among Korean people because of the predominance of Presbyterian, Methodist, and Pentecostal denominations. Compared to 10,000 Presbyterian Churches in Korea, Nazarenes have about 200. Thus, the term "Nazarene" is unfamiliar to all but a few non-Nazarene Koreans, and they are naturally hesitant to join. The insignificance of being a little known denomination is a barrier to a church planter, as demonstrated in Southern California where we have only seven Korean Nazarene churches surviving among 600 other denominational Korean churches.

The second problem is where Nazarene church polity conflicts with Korean culture. Koreans have a village mentality and will naturally flock around a small group leader who is called a Yuji (informal leader). The church must offer a system to hold people together according to their felt needs. In the winter of 1984 the congregation I pastored wanted to ordain a deacon as an elder. But the *Manual* does not allow for any type of lay elder system, only church board members. (It actually doesn't allow for any lay deacon system either). After a discussion with the District Superintendent, the congregation and I obeyed the instructions of the *Manual*. Yet we thought such an elder system was badly needed. Koreans traditionally operate by way of elders as informal leaders. Furthermore, with the Korean corporate personality, an elder system would tend to draw networks of family and friends into the church, leading to greater growth.

The Problem of Worship Facilities

In 1983 a Korean pastor, Yang, started a congregation in the Hollywood Church of the Nazarene, but several months later they asked him to withdraw from the congregation because of what they felt was improper use of the church building. Yang relocated.

In 1987 I made an effort to launch a new work in the San Fernando Valley, but I was unable to use the church building in any church of the Nazarene in the San Fernando Valley. There was one reason after another.

One church in Northridge offered their facility for two hours use on Sunday only. For six months we struggled to survive then finally abandoned the effort.

I strongly felt that there was a deep misunderstanding between American culture and Korean culture in the Church of the Nazarene.

Korean churches operate under the leadership of Americans who do not know Korean culture or worldview, and secondly, Korean pastors are pastoring Korean Churches of the Nazarene without knowing about American culture, language, or worldview Thus, both sides are offended by differences rooted in culture and worldview.

The Korean Church of the Nazarene in Korea does not have to operate cross culturally nor does it operate under leadership of another culture.

But Korean pastors in America suffer from their own lack of understanding as well as that of their host congregations. Some American churches have striven to understand the culture of the Korean congregations, but the gap seems to be too wide. The congregations, the pastors and superintendents of both cultures find themselves caught in unexpected and recurring problems.

The Problem of Korean Immigrant Families

The crisis of identity is a genuine problem of each immigrant family and individual due to changes in social and cultural contexts of the first generation of immigrants. Clifford Geertz points out three areas of chaos, which threaten our sense of meaning in life: bafflement, suffering and injustice (quoted in Hiebert 1987:58).

Bafflement is a pervasive problem among Korean immigrants. The first generation has a major crisis of identity because of radical

9

social, cultural and linguistic changes, and conflicts with the American culture, language, and social system.

The 1.5-generation Koreans speak English as their second language; they struggle to adjust and adapt to the cultural and social context at school and at work. Their bafflement is endless, since they face new values and themes of culture, which induce conflict, insecurity, and loneliness with frustration and anxiety at being a foreigner who can never quite feel like a first class citizen.

My ultimate purpose is to communicate the timeless Christian message to this generation of Korean immigrants in America, according to their context, without diluting it. In the following chapter I will give an overview of the history of the Nazarene Church in order to study its formative period and its conventions in terms of church doctrine and government. Reflecting on the formative era I purpose to shed light on the role of context for understanding the doctrine of holiness.

Chapter 2

THE RISE OF THE CHURCH OF THE NAZARENE U.S.A.

My purpose in this Nazarene history section is not to provide a thorough history of the church but to focus on the roots of the theological and organizational patterns of the Church of the Nazarene. It has always been what may be called a culture-specific church, which means that it arose from distinctly American roots resulting in an ethos that is, in most respects, indigenous to the American social and religious situation which existed around the turn of the century. Thus, I wish to demonstrate how historical roots have shaped the denomination.

The Holiness Movement: History of Formation

On the eve of the American Civil War, in the fall of 1857, a great revival swept over the United States called "The Second Evangelical Awakening" (Edwin Orr 1981:25). A preliminary prayer movement was followed by a holiness emphasis on preaching, which brought mass conversion and revival. Churches everywhere held special evangelistic services and half a million individuals professed conversion. Laymen and ministers of all denominations took part and the revival movement spread from city to city and from town to town. It was a time of revival for

Anglican, Baptist, Congregational, Disciples, Reformed and other evangelical bodies throughout Europe and North America as well as Australia and Africa (Orr 1981:25). "It also inspired hundreds of Christians to pursue deeper spiritual experiences and seek holiness of heart and life" (Timothy Smith 1962:11).

The Holiness Movement came out of this awakening as Timothy Smith describes it, "The deepening of moral conviction hardened resistance against the sin of slavery, soon to be done away with in the Civil War, and rejuvenated as well the crusades against intemperance, Sabbath desecration, and neglect of the poor" (Smith 1962:11). As Kenneth Scott Latourette describes it, "There were also similar groups which in one combination or another had the word 'Holiness' in their title and spoke of a second 'blessing' beyond conversion and ensuing perfection of life" (1975:1260).

The American Civil War brought drastic changes. The nation became industrialized, urbanized and modernized out of its simple agricultural environment. Churches grew wealthy and neglected the poor. Vinson Synan clearly points out the context:

> All churches experienced the challenge to established religion thrown down by Darwinism, socialism, higher criticism, and the social gospel.... The rise of big industrial empires with all the attendant evils of monopolies, unequal distribution of wealth, and political corruption, posed a special dilemma to Protestantism.... The years that followed the Civil War were characterized by a moral depression in America. Returning soldiers with "battlefield ethics" entered not only the house of business but also the halls of government and sanctuaries of the churches (1971:33–34).

Smith wrote that prominent pastors believed that Christian churches were spiritually in crisis as was the secular society. The medication for the corruption of morality and spirituality was a return to the faith of their founders. Their concerns of deeper spiritual life and higher Christian life began to spread over the denominations as water soaking into dry ground.

Phoebe Palmer, wife of a New York City physician, conducted a "Tuesday Prayer Meeting for Promotion of Holiness" and was influential in the New York region. Different camp meetings, revival services and holiness gatherings also rose up in many cities. The Holiness Movement grew nationwide (1962:12).

Since the Church of the Nazarene came out of the Holiness Movement, one cannot fully comprehend its teaching and doctrine without studying the history of this Movement. It was the result of a spiritual awakening prior to the turn of the century, based on the preaching and teaching of John Wesley. The Holiness Movement was formed by the "come-outers" (i.e., the identity of those who left the Methodist, Congregational, Baptist, and Presbyterian churches) (1962:28–33). In retrospect, it can be said that the Church of the Nazarene is a conceptualized church whose historical origins are similar to John Wesley's original Methodist movement, which had emerged from the Anglican Church two centuries earlier.

The Holiness Movement in the East

Phoebe Palmer was one of the outstanding figures, who conducted her "Tuesday Meeting" for the promotion of Holiness for twenty years. Under Palmer's influence, "The Guide to Holiness" was published in Boston, and "hundreds of Methodist preachers, including two bishops," had holiness experiences (1962:12). The Holiness revival continued in every major denomination under key figures like Charles Finney, Asa Mahan, William Boardman, A.B. Earl, Hannah Whitall Smith, John A. Wood, and John Inkship (*Manual* 1989:16–17). Holiness prayer meetings seemed to be the expression of people's deep-seated desire for revival of their faith, and the number of meetings multiplied.

It is interesting that there were two wings to this Holiness Movement, one that rejected uncontrolled emotions and speaking in "unknown" tongues, and another that embraced both of these phenomena. The Church of the Nazarene belonged to the former wing.

According to Smith, the Nazarene founding fathers were William Howard Hoople (Baptist), Edward F. Walker (Presbyterian), J.0. McClurkan (Cumberland Presbyterian), A.M. Hills and George Sharpe, both Scottish Congregationalists. They were mostly heirs of Keswick or Oberlin movements, both of which leaned toward congregational and independent church

13

government (1962:21). The roots of the Holiness Movement started with revivals in reaction to the lax American church. Thus we can see it as a contextualized movement raising up a new church for Americans of that era.

The Holiness Movement spread through the East, West, and Midwest. The history of the Nazarenes in the East begins with the People's Evangelical Church, organized on July 21, 1887, in South Providence, Rhode Island, followed by the Mission Church in Lynn, Massachusetts, on November 25, 1888. In March 1889, representatives from these churches and other evangelical holiness groups organized the Central Evangelical Holiness Association. Within the next year the Emmanuel Mission Church and Bethany Mission Church were organized (*Manual* 1989:17–18).

In December 1895, delegates from Utica Avenue Pentecostal Tabernacle, Bedford Avenue Pentecostal Church, and Emmanuel Pentecostal Tabernacle formed the Association of Pentecostal Churches of America (Manual 1989:18). The new churches were organized in order to meet the needs resulting from the people's new context.

The Holiness Movement in the West: Church of the Nazarene
The beginnings of the Church of the Nazarene on the West coast are largely synonymous with Phineas Bresee, who desired to preach the holiness message to the poor.

***Phineas Bresee and the First Church of the Nazaren*e.** In Southern California Bresee became the pastor of Peniel Mission in Los Angeles. The Methodist Church removed him from the presiding eldership in 1892 because he worked interdenominationally at the mission (1962:106). The *Peniel Herald* defined the Mission as being "thoroughly evangelical but entirely undenominational" (Oct. 1894, quoted in Smith 1962:50). Bresee intended to carry out both the cultural and evangelistic mandates through the Mission's interdenominational and evangelical mission work. It ministered to the poor who were being neglected by the mainline denominations of his time.

After Bresee began to serve the Mission, some of his friends distributed printed matter to promote holiness doctrine and evangelistic city mission work. The holiness people gathered in October 1895 and formed the First Church of the Nazarene with

135 charter members. "The name of the church was chosen in honor of the Lord Jesus Christ who, according to Matthew 2:23, was called a 'Nazarene,'" writes M.E. Redford (1948:47).

One of the founding fathers, Widney explained the choice of the name was meant to symbolize "the toiling, lowly mission of Christ" (1962:111). The first Nazarene literature ever printed was a flyer to advertise the meetings at Red Men's Hall, which read:

> The Church of the Nazarene is a simple, primitive church, a church of the people and for the people. It has no new doctrines, only the old, old Bible truths: It seeks to discard all superfluous forms and ecclesiasticism and go back to the plain, simple words of Christ. It is not a mission, but a church with a mission. It is a banding together of hearts that have found the peace of God, and which now in their gladness go out to carry the message of the unsearchable riches of the gospel of Christ to other suffering, discouraged, sin sick souls. Its mission is to everyone that hungers for cleansing from Sin (Quoted in Smith 1862:111).

Bresee has been correctly called by many "the founder of the Nazarenes." As a presiding elder of a Methodist Church, he actually founded the first Church of the Nazarene, which still stands on West 3rd Street in Los Angeles. The first *Manual* reveals the founder's heart for the poor:

> We were convinced that houses of worship should be plain and cheap, to save from financial burdens, and that everything should say welcome to the poor.... The gospel comes to a multitude without money and without price, and the poorest of the poor are entitled to a front seat at the Church of the Nazarene (Quoted in Smith 1962:114).

This demonstrates that Bresee stood against fine church buildings and clericalism, and promoted a humble and plain place of worship. He simplified the worship format while focusing on the Holy Spirit and sanctification. Redford described the fervent praise and prayer of that church, "The songs of praise and shouts of victory were distasteful to the irreligious owners of the building, and the Nazarenes were requested to find another place to worship" (1948:47). He explained that they secured a larger and more suitable place on North Main Street later. He described the genuine and humble beginning by the pitching of a tent, a tabernacle church of the Nazarene:

> Instead of a cornerstone's being laid for the new building a large spike was started in the appropriate place and each member of the church took the hammer and helped to drive it. The driving of the spike was done at intervals of prayers, testimonies, and songs of praise (1948:48).

Also he expressed the motivation of the new church, quoting Dr. Bresee's words, "We do not desire costly churches. We do desire the power and glory of the manifest divine presence. We rejoice in Him. In this board tabernacle the poor are made rich, the sorrowing to rejoice. Heaven greets and fills our souls" (1948:48–49).

The new church essentially contextualized the gospel for relevant and effective communication to a particular audience. This stimulated growth. In a biography of Bresee, Girvin records:

> A company of tourists one day, leaving the city for their eastern homes, were overjoyed to tell what they had seen in Los Angeles, and one of them asked: "Did you go to the Church of the Nazarene?" The other answered, "No, we heard about it, and intended to go, but in some way were hindered." The first rejoined: "Well, you ought to have gone. You never saw anything like it. The people sang and shouted and stood up and said they were sanctified, and it was the greatest thing you ever saw" (quoted in Redford 1948:49).

The new church rapidly grew to 350 members in one year, and over the next eight years acquired 1500 members and throngs of churches (Smith 1962:112).

Growth of the Church of the Nazarene in the West. As a sturdy oak grows from a small acorn, so the church began to grow from a small, lowly group of people. As the wind of holy fire expanded the vision of Bresee, the work of holiness in the key cities spread. New churches were established in Berkeley, Oakland, Elysian Heights, and South Pasadena, while "a continuous revival prevailed at the First Church of the Nazarene in

Los Angeles, attracting large attendance" (Redford 1948:50). Bresee preached the gospel simply to meet people's needs, and before he knew it, a new denomination began taking form.

In 1898, a meeting of delegates from various churches issued the first *Manual* (doctrine and practices) of the Church of the Nazarene. The general rules for the Christian life (both negative and positive) in 1898 were almost identical with those in the 1948 *Manual* (Redford 1948:56), and the 1989 *Manual* continues to be much the same. Considering the vast changes in North American culture one might question if Nazarene doctrine and practice has changed enough to meet changing contexts. And considering the worldwide expansion of the church, the unchanging nature of the *Manual* also suggests that North American rules and practices are relevant and normative for the rest of the world. But given widely divergent cultural contexts, general rules for Americans may be difficult to apply to Koreans or other ethnic groups.

In October 1899, Bresee was elected as General Superintendent of the Church of the Nazarene, and he sent out a call for a kind of general assembly. Soon the Nazarene Publishing Company was formed in Los Angeles for the purpose of printing the Nazarene and other holiness literature.

In October 1902, C.W. Ruth, an evangelist with the Holiness Movement in the East, organized the Church of the Nazarene in Spokane, Washington. In 1903, churches in Utah, Nebraska, Idaho, Minnesota, Illinois, and Washington transferred in from other denominations (Redford 64–65; Cf. Smith 1962:131).

It is notable that in the beginning, Bresee was not inclined toward ecclesiasticism, but in the end he had to form ecclesiastical districts for the administration of the general church. This ecclesiastical system is entirely based on the patterns and values of European/American worldviews and social systems, with democracy playing a prominent role.

The Holiness Movement in the South

The Civil War had left deep wounds in the hearts of the people in the South. The socio-economic situation had been devastated by the defeat. This was a contributing factor to people's openness to the Holiness Movement.

"By the 1880s, many Cumberland Presbyterian pastors were stressing the doctrine of the baptism of the Holy Spirit as a 'second blessing,' and supporting holiness camp meetings and revival in their communities" (George McCulloch quoted in Smith 1962:152). The major reason for the difference between the Holiness Movement here and in other areas of the nation was the large segment of the Methodist Episcopal Church, which was against the doctrine of entire sanctification. It caused a series of local crises for those individual preachers who believed in the baptism of the Holy Spirit.

In the 1890s, as the Holiness Movement spread, Methodist elders were facing their own crisis of being ousted from their ministries. The problem came to a climax in 1894 after the General Conference adopted a rule forbidding any Methodist preacher or evangelist to hold meetings within parish boundaries without the local pastor's approval. This action quickened the formation of a new church in Milan, Tennessee, which in 1908 united with the Nazarenes (Smith 1962:152).

The New Testament Church and Mary Lee Harris

In 1890, Robert Lee Harris, a west Texan and cowboy evangelist returned to America from independent mission work in Liberia. In November 1893, the West Tennessee Methodist Episcopal Conference labeled his work as being that of an unauthorized, self-styled evangelist and "in the main an evil of great magnitude" (1962:153). So Harris organized the New Testament Church of Christ. He contracted tuberculosis and before his death encouraged his wife and several other women to preach. Smith describes Harris's ministry:

> Harris added baptism by pouring; the Methodist doctrine of sanctification as a second work of grace; and the renouncing all forms of worldliness: sinful amusement, extravagance in dress, the wearing of jewelry, membership in secret societies, and the use of opium, tobacco, or intoxicating drinks (1962:154).

These rules were in a sense contextualized for the movement of the church in that day. They show continuity with the general rules of the Nazarene *Manual* all the way up to today. However some can never be seen as relevant to Korean culture, as we shall see.

From 1894 to 1901, small churches began to spread through west Tennessee, Arkansas, northern Alabama, and sections of Texas under preacher Mary Harris, the wife of the founder, She traveled back and forth conducting revival meetings in Texas and Tennessee. She encouraged women to be active in ministry, and she herself organized a dozen small congregations. Harris remarried, taking the name Cagle, and settled down as pastor of a church in Buffalo Gap, promoting annual holiness camp meetings. She was a forceful and influential leader in the southwest Holiness Movement long before men began to exert leadership. Thus women arose in leadership despite prejudice against women preachers in Cumberland and Church of Christ circles (1962:158–159).

In December 1899, a business meeting of the church at Milan under the chairmanship of R.B. Mitchum took up several questions which were of general interest to the entire movement: unity with other holiness movements, supplying the pastors, and the ordination of women. As a result, Cagle (formerly Harris) and a Mrs. Sheeks were ordained (1962:156–157).

In 1902, in response to numerous suggestions, Cagle sent out a call to the different congregations recruiting delegates to the general meeting at Buffalo Gap. The delegates from eleven churches, sixteen ministers and eight laymen, were noticeably preoccupied with protecting congregational and laymen's rights in deciding statements of doctrine and guidance for the congregations. Later union with the Nazarenes replaced council leadership with full-fledged superintendency (Smith 1962:158–60).

This procedure explains how Nazarene congregational structures came to exist in the Southwest, which held a distinctly different view of the leadership structure from than that of a Korean village. Yet the history of Mary Harris's and other women's leadership is encouraging and applicable to the Korean context.

The Holiness Movement in Texas

According to Smith, a Texas Holiness association, organized in the fall of 1878 conducted annual camp meetings in the triangle between Corsicana, Dallas, and Waco. The Free Methodist Church soon established a foothold in this area. Among the Methodists, The Northwest Texas Holiness Association flourished after 1885 (1962:159).

In 1888, the first holiness churches in Texas were organized by Thomas and Dennis Rodgers from California. And in 1899 the Holiness Association of Texas was formed. Two years later the first Independent Holiness church was organized at Alstyne, Texas, by C.B. Jernigan (*Manual* 1989:18–19).

In 1898, E.C. DeJernett and Jernigan summoned a convention to provide a home for scorned, churchless holiness people of the South. In 1899 a young minister, B.A. Cordell, bought land and donated it for a college at Peniel. That September, the Texas Holiness University started with twenty-seven students.

The Form and Plan of Organization

Jernigan and others met in Greenville and slowly moved forward to gain wider support. In 1901, they prepared a constitution and statement of doctrine ratified at Peniel.

In 1904, the annual council of the Independent Holiness Church did not further develop any permanent organization. At Rising Star, Texas, the legal representatives of the Independent Holiness Church and the New Testament Church of Christ joined together.

A joint committee framed the *Manual* and statement of doctrine and basis of union. The union was fully consummated at Pilot Point, Texas, in November 1905, and the united body adopted the name "Holiness Church of Christ" (*Manual* 1989:19).

The Holiness Church of Christ, 1905–1908

The Holiness Church of Christ recognized the urgency of an educational institution for preachers and rescue workers. The Bible Institute at Pilot Point was started by the council, which ratified the documents of the church at Rising Star.

Due to dissatisfaction with the regional and sectarian separation of the holiness movement, leaders of holiness churches began appealing for the union of all holiness churches. These appeals paved the way to success in bringing the eastern and western churches together.

Union of East and West

Finally, representatives of the churches in the East and the West met and discussed unity of the church. They set up the principles and rules for unity. The experience of sanctification in a second blessing was the primary distinction for their unity. They named the church the "Pentecostal Church of the Nazarene" (Smith 1962:215).

When these representatives met, they also invited southern representatives. Jernigan and Scott found difficulty in persuading the different groups in the South, because of their many strong leaders. After two full discussions covering the reports, they voted to request new articles because some of them saw little use for the former Methodist system of presiding elders (1962:216). Actually the early Nazarene carried the *Manual* borrowed heavily from the old Methodist *Book of Discipline* (1962:216,222).

They requested the addition of articles pertaining to tobacco and divine healing. In addition, they approved a motion for the provision in the marriage ritual for the discontinuance of rings (1962:216).

Pilot Point Heritage: The Birth of the Nazarenes

In October 1908, the second assembly was held, and on the 13th they approved the unity of the two organizations. Smith said, "So the Nazarenes became one people, North, South, East, and West" (220). Pilot Point is significant for two reasons: First, it signified an "acceleration of the trend away from associations and independent churches toward a fully organized denominational fellowship." Second, it affirmed the church's "unity in essentials and its determination to maintain liberty in all other areas" (Smith 1962:221). Thus Pilot Point, the church's birthplace, became its historical center. Redford records:

> The numerical strength of the united church, as given by the official minutes of the Second General assembly held at Pilot Point, in Texas, in 1908, reported that were 228 churches with a combined membership of 10,414, with 7,780 members of Sunday

School and 523 members of the young peoples' society. The total value of property was placed at $559,953. During the previous year, the amount of $140,756 was raised by the combined church for all purposes. Thus Pilot Point, the church's birthplace, became its historical center (1948:152).

The Pentecostal Mission, a zealous group that sent pastors and teachers to Cuba, Guatemala, Mexico, and India, joined with the Pentecostal Church of the Nazarene in February 1915 (*Manual* 1989:21–22).

The rising Pentecostal movement propagated the practice of speaking in tongues, but the Nazarene church took a stand against it. Thus in November 1919, the church dropped the word "Pentecostal" from its name in order to avoid identification with the Pentecostal movement. Thus it has been known as the Church of the Nazarene since that date (Smith 1962:320). Currently it is the largest holiness denomination in the United States (Synan 1971:145). Subsequently the Holiness Movement and the Nazarenes continued to expand into the Midwest, through Minnesota, the Dakotas, and Montana.

Internationally as of 1990, the Church of the Nazarene has 9,708 churches, 861,110 members, 11,207 ordained ministers, 4,419 licensed ministers, and 608 missionaries. The international headquarters of the Church of the Nazarene is located near Kansas City, Missouri.

Church Doctrine and Government

As its history indicates, the Church of the Nazarene was born a contextualized church designed to meet the needs of the people. As the holiness movement advocated, the Church of the Nazarene promoted holiness theology, emphasizing the doctrine of entire sanctification. It endorsed entire sanctification in its manual as a major doctrine, and formulated practices setting high moral and ethical standards of conduct, which were supposed to be reflections of the contextual problems.

When the East and West churches united to become the Pentecostal Church of the Nazarene, both churches agreed on the essential doctrines. Since the church was born out of the union of congregations from East and West, the church needed to adopt and establish a government for that particular context. This foundation subsequently influenced the polity of local churches.

Formulation of Doctrines and Practices

A joint committee was formed to produce a denominational manual and doctrinal statement. "The first Nazarene *Manual* set forth a simplified version of the 'General Rules,' which the Discipline of the Methodist churches had contained for decades" (Smith 1962:115). The basis of union of the Church of the Nazarene was the doctrines of justification by faith and entire sanctification subsequent to justification. "Both churches recognized that the right of church membership rests upon experience and that persons who have been born of the Spirit are entitled to its privileges" (*Manual* 1985:17).

These people of the North and South were quite different from each other, coming from different backgrounds in ideas, education and in training. Yet as all of them came from an American cultural context, when forming doctrine and polity they could not foresee the needs of the vastly different cultural contexts into which the church would later move.

Entire Sanctification. The essential holiness doctrine is entire sanctification, through the second blessing of the Holy Spirit. Jernigan wrote in his editorial in *Holiness Evangel* in 1906 "Holiness of heart and life was made the basis of the union, with liberty to all on non-essentials." (Smith 1962:215). The 1989 Nazarene *Manual* described the doctrine of entire sanctification as:

> that act of God subsequent to regeneration, by which believers are made free from original sin, or depravity and brought in to a site of entire devotement to God, and holy obedience of love made perfect. It is wrought by the baptism with the Holy Spirit, and comprehends in one experience the cleansing of the heart from sin and the abiding, indwelling presence of the Holy Spirit empowering the believers for life and service. Entire Sanctification is provided by the blood of Jesus, is wrought instantaneously by faith, preceded by entire consecration; and to this work and state of grace the Holy Spirit bears witness (34).

It is the work of the Holy Spirit to purify the believer from inward sin. This means that the inbred sin, which resulted from Adam's fall, is changed to perfect love toward God and man. This doctrine calls for a life fully committed to Jesus Christ, and the pursuit of a life of obedience and victory in Christ.

The experience of entire sanctification also is known by various terms which represent its different phases, such as "Christian perfection," "perfect love," "heart purity," "the baptism with the Holy Spirit," "the fullness of the blessing," and "Christian holiness." The distinction is then made between "heart purity" and Christian maturity. The problem is in how a Christian perceives "heart purity" and expresses a life of holiness in one's cultural context. Smith cites one of Bresee' s articles, "Legalism Overdone," addressing the problems of expecting young Christians to conform to strict standards of dress (1962:216).[1]

General Rules and Special Rules. The Nazarene *Manual* deals with the general rules in Part Two under the Church section then further cites special rules in Part Three. The present rules for the general Christian life in the church are dealt with both negatively and positively. The general rules essentially advocate fundamental Christian ethics and are more or less relevant across cultures.

Regarding special rules, the Manual rightly states the attempt to apply biblical principles such that they are understood "within a variety of cultures." And it acknowledges that "no catalog, however inclusive, can hope to encompass all forms of evil throughout the world" (1989:47). The subsequent rules in the Manual are relevant to North America and to a large extent other cultures. For example, the following are among the prohibitions:

> entertainment ventures and media productions including the motion picture theatre [cinema], except films produced by Christian organizations; television programs, VCR tapes, and drama which produce, promote, or feature the violent, the sensual, the pornographic, the profane, or the occultic...lotteries and other forms of gambling...membership in oath-bound secret orders or societies...all forms of social dancing...the use of intoxicating liquor as beverage...using illicit drugs (1989:48).

While these rules are applicable to Koreans, issues exceedingly more significant to Koreans are not addressed. No rules are found pertaining to ancestral veneration or to shamanistic practices or to fortune telling, geomancy, or concubines—all of which are deeply imbued in the lives of non-Christian Korean immigrants. Turning away from these practices is the precise evidence of conversion, and thus it is in these areas where one may measure a person's true Christian commitment.

That these issues do not appear in the *Manual* is quite understandable. Commendably, the *Manual* encourages Nazarenes on an international scale to "earnestly seek the aid of the Spirit in cultivating a sensitivity to evil which transcends the mere letter of the law...." (*Manual* 1989:47). This is a very positive and important statement for Koreans when dealing with culturally related issues not dealt with in the special rules.

Problems occur, however, when American pastors expect their Korean congregations to abide by the *Manual*'s special rules without being sensitive to the deep underlying significance and meaning of turning away from sins almost unknown to Americans but highly significant for Koreans. Thus they may seek to stress prohibitions in the *Manual* while overlooking other sins far more serious to the Korean church. The misunderstanding and resulting conflict is essentially cultural.

The problem is not with the *Manual*. Rather it is on one hand the problem of first generation Korean immigrants unable to adapt to the *Manual* as is, and on the other an inflexible imposition of the North American *Manual* on first generation Korean immigrants.

I have summarized the beginnings and the development of the Church of the Nazarene, which will lead us to study the cultural and worldview differences that are becoming increasingly significant. I shall reserve suggestions and recommendations on contextual problems until the final chapter.

Chapter 3

CONTEXTUALIZATION

As has been said the motivation and purpose for looking at contextualization in this study results from the frustration that came from my own attempts at cross-cultural church planting and pastoral ministry. Working with the Korean immigrants under American leadership, I encountered an unbridgeable gap between two worldviews, American and Korean. The barriers between these two worldviews produced problems in receiving members and establishing lay leaders in developing a Korean immigrant church.

Therefore, I determined to discover the relevant factors and find out what we can do about them. This led to the study of the cultures and worldviews with the hope that contextualization would provide answers. In order to do so I have briefly reviewed the history of the Church of the Nazarene in order to highlight the culture and context of its formative era. I am convinced that it is deeply rooted in the worldview of a particular era of American history.

In moving toward recommendations for the Korean Church of the Nazarene, I shall first of all present a general overview of conceptualization then deal with the leading models in order to suggest appropriate ways of thinking about contextualization for the specific problems raised by the Korean Nazarene Church in America.

General Overview

The term contextualization, which has been around for about two decades, was given official sanction by The Theological Educational Fund (TEF), which developed a working definition in 1972. "Contextualization is the capacity to respond meaningfully to the gospel within the framework of one's own situation" (Coe and Sapsezian 1972:20). Contextualization is not the translation or adaptation of an existing theology into different periods or geographic regions. It is not transplanting western theology for Third World people. It is doing theology in the context without diluting or syncretizing the gospel.

It starts with God communicating with people within their own contexts for salvific purposes. God spoke to Adam and Eve directly in the Garden of Eden, then through Moses, the prophets and eventually through the incarnation of Christ. The Gospel of Matthew was written to the Hebrews of Eden, then through Moses, the prophets and eventually through the incarnation of Christ. The Gospel of Matthew was written to the Hebrews emphasizing Messianic fulfillment; Luke was written to gentiles in a Hellenistic culture. Thus, long before the word "contextualization," ever appeared, it had been a reality in the Bible. The term "contextualization" has been frequently debated theologically since it was coined by TEF.

Missiologists had used terms such as: adaptation, accommodation, indigenous, inculturation, and more recently, the incarnation of theology, local theology, ethnotheology, and contextualization.[1]

Reformation theology and Wesleyan theology are, in fact, conceptualizations of theology. Acts 15 describes how the early church thought through issues of the gentiles, making it evident that God is interested in communicating His message of salvation within a people's life context. For Daniel von Allmen, contextualization is an attempt to express the fact that the situation of theology in a process of self-adaptation to a new or changing context is the same in Europe as in Asia or in Africa (1975:37).

Von Allmen perceives that self-adaptation to a changing context is the opposite of deliberately changing the system of society as liberation theology attempts to do. God demonstrated

Himself as the model of contextualization, coming into the world in human flesh to communicate with His people. After a long history of law and prophets, He came into the life situation of the people, living with them in their context in order to communicate a message, reveal Himself and bring salvation.

The Christ event interacts with all people throughout time and contexts for His redemptive purpose. Likewise, the forms of communication have been changed through the generations and centuries, yet the meaning of the content is unchanged, because "Jesus Christ is the same yesterday, today and forever" (Heb.13:8).[2] Kraft comments, "Our God is a communicating God.... He no sooner had created humans than he began to talk to them" (1989:123).

Kraft borrowed Eugene Nida's term, "Christian Ethnotheology," to describe the attempt, which combines anthropological insights with theological principles for the purpose of an interpretive approach of theologizing in context (1979:13). The basis is that God's communication of His message with his people is contextualized within the language and the culture (1989:125).

Since Kraft centers on communication, he approaches contextualization with a translation model, which seeks a dynamic equivalents to the New Testament Church for the specific culture. The assumption, therefore, is that we must communicate to Koreans in Los Angeles differently from Koreans in Korea, even though while in Los Angeles, they are also Korean.

Louis J. Luzbetak proposes the word "accommodation" for contextualization defining it as "the respectful, prudent, scientifically and theologically sound adjustment of a church to the native culture in attitude, outward, and practical apostolic approach" (1970:341). He demands a more perfect understanding of the gospel and the real world for better theologizing in context. The Korean Church of the Nazarene in the U.S.A. is not located in Korean indigenous culture; rather, it is among Koreans in the setting of a foreign culture. Its context is neither monocultural nor monolingual. People have their cultural roots, yet they are breathing in American culture.

As von Allman reminded us, contextualization attempts to restructure theology in a process of adaptation to new or changing situations. The Korean Church of the Nazarene in California is in the process of change, but even more significant than the process of change are the inherent differences between the two churches' cultures.

James Buswell uses the word "inculturation" to explain the process of communicating Christian truth in linguistic symbols and forms by using that culture's own analogies, illustrations, forms and principles of gospel communication to make the gospel message intelligible to the receivers (1978:90–91). Since culture lies in the hearts of people, this insight is very important. Yet, context extends beyond cultural forms and linguistic symbols to include political, socio-economic and demographic settings.

Rene Padilla gave an important presentation at the Willowbank Consultation on the gospel and the Culture, held in January 1978. He called attention to the need for dialogue with contemporary cultural contexts as well as the Biblical text (Padilla 1983:80–84). As Lesslie Newbigin points out, "The value of the word contextualization is that it suggests the placing of the gospel in total context of a culture at a particular moment, a moment that is shaped by the past and looks to the future" (1986:2).

Rather than ignoring or condemning the culture, it should be respected, used and transformed. This is to observe, in passing, that Korean people can be Korean Nazarenes, but they cannot be American Nazarenes. My own definition for the contextualization of Christian theology is that it is a dynamic process in a particular time and place by which biblical truths are allowed to be expressed and communicated in word and deed, in ways understandable and meaningful to the receptors, while avoiding syncretism and dilution of the message.

Inherent in this process is submission to Scripture as the authoritative Word of God, sensitivity and obedience to the leading of the Holy Spirit, and interaction between the bearer of gospel truth and the receptors' context, thus allowing the message to be conveyed in ways natural to them.

Effective contextualization results in the spiritual transformation of receptors so that they live under the Lordship of Jesus Christ, while at the same time they retain their cultural identity in self-perception, in theologizing, and in Christian practice.

God Himself communicated the Gospel of Matthew to the Jews in a Messianic way and the Gospel of Luke to the gentiles as the Son of God, as Savior. In Matthew the word "Kingdom of Heaven" was written to the Jews, while the expression "Kingdom of God" was more acceptable for the gentiles in Luke.

The Need for Contextualization

The Christian message is the content and church is the container of the message. The message of Christian truth is absolute, but the church is clothed in culture. Allan Tippett points out: "The greatest methodological issue faced by the Christian mission in our day is how to carry out the Great Commission in a multi-cultured world, with a gospel that is both truly Christian in content and culturally significant in form" (quoted in Donald Hohensee 1980:37).

This is because any theology is built on the basis of the worldview of the working theologians, which illustrates that while Christ is absolute, Christian theology develops from a particular perspective or point of view. Thus, the church's interpretation is not free from bias.

Therefore, Kraft asserts that we have to take into consideration three elements of Christian cross-cultural communication: The culture of the message, the culture of the communicator from which he interprets, and the culture of the hearer or receptor (1979:46). This implies that the contexts in which the original message was written, theologized and perceived are all different and should each be taken seriously.

Keesing and Keesing point out how our perception, judgment, value, logic, and conceptualization are governed by our culture:

> To view other people's ways of life in terms of our own cultural glasses is called ethnocentrism. Becoming conscious of and analytical about our own cultural glasses is a painful business. We do it best by learning about other peoples' glasses. Although we can never take our glasses off to find out what the world is "really like," or try looking through anyone else's without ours on as well, we can at least learn a good deal about our own prescription (1971:21).

30

This leads us to an assumption that there is no sacred culture or method, ordained by God, which can be unanimously applicable in the world. Some years before the discussion on conceptualization, Latourette articulated the need for indigeneity: "To be indigenous, Christianity shall become so rooted among a people that they shall feel it to be their own and not something alien" (1940:429). He suggests dynamic interaction of the gospel in terms of the traditional culture and expects young churches to take their context seriously.

The term "indigenous" had many of the same connotations and concerns in missiology as contextualization. But Charles Taber and Shoki Coe were among those who showed in 1970's that indigeneity tends to be static, that is, once formed it tends not to change, while contextualization is dynamic, that is, open to review and modification as part of the process. Taber writes that conceptualization not only extends but also corrects the error and the biases of the term, "indigenous" (1979:27).

We can see contextualization in God's dealing with His people in the Old Testament and even more clearly in the incarnation through Jesus' ministry. He ordered Moses to build the tabernacle, in which He could dwell among Jewish people while they wandered for forty years in the wilderness. The tabernacle was light enough to carry and mobile enough to pitch and fold. He knew His peoples' context. Later He ordered Solomon to build His dwelling place as a stone temple, because Israel was settled in one country.

Eventually Jesus came in the flesh and made his personal dwelling among us. While he was on earth he ministered to people according to their felt needs. He made the lame walk, gave sight to the blind, cast out demons and offered freedom to the poor as well as the rich, while He was preaching Good News and teaching the scriptures. Jesus exemplified through Himself how to approach individuals in terms of the felt needs of their contexts.

Through the Holy Spirit he moved his dwelling within us and we ourselves became the temple of the Holy Spirit. At each step he contextualized his dwelling place according to God's plans and his people's changing situations.

Models of Contextualization

Different models have been developed in the last decade. They all have differences, commonalities, strengths, and weaknesses. They start with different assumptions and different methodologies, yet by and large, they have the same goal of fulfilling the Great Commission.

I will briefly review the leading models to show the variety of ways contextualization can be carried out. All are commonly committed to the communication of a relevant message to a given people and to the development of an authentic experience of Christian truth in the growth of the body of believers.[3]

The Anthropological Model

This model lays particular stress on listening to the culture. The culture is learned and is the storehouse, which gives people values and themes of life. People are born in the culture and immersed in the culture; they learn to meet essential needs according to the culture. The culture is the grid through which people look and interpret reality. According to Robert McAfee Brown this model is categorized by three criteria, which affect the content (Brown 1977:170–174 and Stephen Bevans 1985:188).

The general presuppositions of the anthropological models are: First, the goodness of culture and human nature is recognized and reaffirmed. Culture is not only the material through which the Christian message is expressed, but the message is also discovered within the culture. Second, as a consequence, culture is seen having no need of adaptation or accommodation, because culture is free from demonic elements. Third, the culture is considered unique and should not be intruded on by any theology. Fourth, the model concludes that culture is normative and genuine and is found in the language, behavior and experience of ordinary people. Through analysis of a people's rituals and language a genuine contextualization can take place.

The fundamental characteristic, then, of the anthropological model is that culture is the starting point, which sets the agenda for theology. The anthropological model recognizes that culture influenced the writing of Scripture and documents of tradition and these elements are difficult to separate from the essence and content of revelation.

The Translation Model

This commonly used model originates from the Bible and the discipline of translation and aims to transmit a message that is true to the original message as well as to the contemporary hearer's or reader's situation. It, therefore, provides meaningful interpretations in terms of their particular language and culture.

Eugene Nida states the importance of this model: "Translation is not merely conveying information, but expressing in an equivalent style something of the emotionally charged character of the original" (1954:221). Kraft writes:

> The new aim is to go beyond the focus of the earlier translation theory. There is still focus on words, grammar, and expression-but for the purpose of building a communicational bridge between the author and contemporary hearer. And building such a bridge must take into account the cultural and linguistic involvement of both the ancient author and contemporary hearer (1979:270).

This model is dealt with comprehensively in Kraft's *Christianity in Culture*. Kraft developed the Dynamic Equivalence Model from Bible translation. The model holds to several presuppositions in the theologizing process.

Bible translation does not mean translating word for word, or literal translation (which Kraft calls, "formal correspondence") (1979:264). Literal translations of the Word are not capable of conveying the original message because of cultural and linguistic differences between biblical and contemporary cultures.

Dynamic or functionally equivalent words or idioms are necessary for communication of the message. Thus, Kraft holds that, because of the requirements of the target language and culture, some degree of paraphrasing can be included in a translation to make it intelligible and impactful while still legitimately calling it a translation (1979:272). Kraft clearly sees the translation model as being one of dynamic equivalence. The essence of Christianity is supra-cultural.

The translation model holds that the supra-cultural message can be separated from the cultural elements of language and from cultural concepts in that language. The words "absolute truth" and "relative truth" depict the kernel (message) and husk (expression).

The Praxis Model

The praxis model, which is used by those of the more conciliar approach, has usually been identified with liberation theology. Comparing various models, Bevans states,

> If the anthropological model focuses on the cultural identity of the Christian, and if the translation model focuses on Christian identity within a culture, the praxis model focuses on Christian identity within a culture from the point of social change (1985:192).

The Praxis model, however, assumes that the truth can only be realized when social change is produced by the people's participation in the events of their history. Assumptions of the praxis models are as follows:

1. The model presupposes the analysis of social realities within a context or culture, then engages in appropriate action. To do this it demands people's involvement in correcting injustice, oppression, or other dehumanized elements, and influencing the society toward being a more Christian environment. It emphasizes the Bible and Christian tradition in social reality.

2. The praxis model holds that change comes not by cognitive belief but by action. It presupposes that God's revelation is ongoing in history and manifest in social, political and cultural events. As a result, where God is acting, people are also acting as his partners.

3. The praxis model concerns both orthodoxy (right belief) and orthopraxy (right doing). The Conference of Third World Theologians at Dar es Salaam in 1976 reported the following which lays emphasis on the acting out of theology: "No theology is neutral; any theological statement is a political and economic statement as well.... We reject as irrelevant an academic type of theology that is divorced from action" (Quoted in Bevans 1985:192–193).

The Adaptation Model

The Adaptation Model attempts to apply the historical foci of systematic theology into a particular cultural situation. This approach assumes that there is one philosophical framework which all cultures share. Expatriates, in consort with local theologians, will endeavor to develop an implicit philosophy or picture of the worldview of the culture.

This picture will fit into either the category of a philosophical model or a cultural, anthropological description of Western theologies, which becomes a basis for developing a theology.

This model takes culture seriously but often imports foreign elements into the local culture. This model would accept a form of worship, for example, in which Nigerians sing in Latin hymnody, or where the Tridentine Mass is celebrated in urban churches in the People's Republic of China. In other words, foreign categories, philosophical frameworks, and traditions are brought into local theology.

The Synthetic Model

This model brings together features of all the models in order to articulate a new approach. It can be called dialectical in terms of Hegelian methodology and in the way it synthesizes the gospel, Christian tradition, culture, and social change. Therefore, this model presupposes that while a particular culture or context is unique, it also shares elements with other cultures. As a result, the emphasis of this model seeks both cultural uniqueness and dialogue with other cultures.

The synthetic model also assumes anthropological models and translations to be linear and the procedure of the praxis model to be circular or cyclic, which produces the fundamental multi-directional procedure of the synthetic model.

Thus, the synthetic model is dialectic and biological in process. Due to the nature of the synthetic model, it points to the universality of Christianity in a way that opens dialogue with every culture or thought form for its adaptability to Christianity.

The Semiotic Model

Robert Schreiter is the name most associated with this model. The semiotic model attempts to analyze signs and symbols that indicate where change in the society is happening. The term "semiotic" comes from the Greek word section, meaning "sign." This model "listens" to a culture through an analysis of these signs and symbols. Schreiter defines semiotics and it's approach in this way:

> Semiotics studies the sign-system of the culture. It views the culture as a vast communication system, which sends messages (values) throughout an elaborate circuitry (culture patterns, modes of behavior, rules). This circuitry has a number of nodes where the circuits cluster. These points of semiotic density are crucial points where meaning is constructed, where old meanings are judged, where new meanings are formed (1977a:31).

Schreiter's semiotic model assumes revelation is inherent in the context itself, and is in this way similar to the anthropological model. Thus, the model presupposes that Christ can be found in the values, symbols and behavioral patterns of the culture. It is not the communication of absolute truth from outside to people in cultural contexts but the communication of truth already within cultural context on which one builds a local theology. For Schreiter,

> [Culture] represents a way of life for a given time and place, replete with values, symbols, and meanings, reaching out with hopes and dreams, often struggling for a better world. Without a sensitivity to the cultural context, a church and its theology either become a vehicle for outside domination or lapse into Docetism, as though its Lord never became flesh.
> It takes the dynamic interaction of all these three roots—gospel, church, culture-with all they entail about identity and change, to have the makings of local theology (1985:21).

Thus, it is capable of providing the theology of the changing community by taking culture and tradition seriously. Louis Luzbetak points out that Christ will be first experienced and then reborn as a true member of the local society and as full sharer of the local culture (1981:39).

36

Luzbetak further states that the Church "must make Africans into African Christians, Indians into Indian Christians Japanese into Japanese Christians-not into American or European Christians" (1970:344).

The semiotic approach is a complicated process of studying Scripture and tradition, cultural symbols, patterns, and behavior. Only theologians who are intimate with the culture are able to do this.

Criteria for Contextualization

When undergoing the contextualization process, one must pay careful attention to accurate biblical exegesis and relevant theologizing faithful to Scripture. One must pay equally careful attention to accurate understanding of the recipient culture and the worldview of its people, while maintaining a positive, constructive attitude toward them.

The Biblical Basis

The Bible is the self-revelation of God and the source of understanding how God deals with humans in salvation history. David Hesselgrave points out, "the contextualizer must take into account the nature of biblical revelation and also the nature of the scriptures of the various religious traditions" (Hesselgrave and Rommen 1989:128).

Biblical theology deals with contexts of the time and history of God's redemptive activity with His people. Therefore, a biblical foundation is essential for doing theology in context. Harvey Conn points out, "Biblical theology provides a model that, by its very nature, reminds us of the historico-contextual character of our theologizing" (1984:225). Yet the uniqueness of Christian faith lies in the fact that the Bible speaks to everyone in every generation and every situation.

The biblical text is the starting point for understanding the context in which God worked out His salvation among His people in history. In the theologizing process we cannot escape our presuppositions, ideology and understanding about society, cultures, and history; no one can read the Bible without bias. Yet the salvation message is unchanging, and God's redemptive activities are ongoing in changing societies. Therefore, doing theology within the biblical context itself is prerequisite for sound biblical contextualization.

There are pitfalls in placing the context above the text. Over-preoccupation with the relevance of the message relegates the Truth itself to secondary status. Because of this danger we need to know exegetically the meaning of the text in its biblical context.

The primacy of biblical exegesis goes hand in hand with the inspiration and illumination of the Holy Spirit in the process of theologizing. Paul wrote, "No one knows the thoughts of God except the Spirit of God" (1 Cor.2:11); thus, the Spirit's leading is vital to the contextualization process. Padilla points out that, "The Inspired Word externally and the testimony of the Spirit internally are combined together in a single witness to the reality of God and his saving power" (1983:83).

The Holy Spirit who inspired Scripture is the same Spirit who illumines us in understanding God's message, which is the plumb line of divine inspiration. Thus, without biblical foundation, contextualization has no validity, and without the Spirit's illumination, contextualization is limited to human methodology.

The Cultural Basis

People are born and learn to behave in cultural ways before they are even conscious of it. Adams Hoebel describes culture as an "integrated system of learned behavior patterns which are characteristic of the members of a society and which are not the result of biological inheritance" (1972:6).

Each individual is born into a particular socio-cultural context. Therefore, their perception of reality is dependent on their mental construct gained as a member of that society. Culture guides a person like a road map guides a traveler. Therefore, we need to recognize that our interpretation of the Christian message depends in part on our specific cultural perception. Gilliland explains clearly:

> Contextualization focuses on categories of truth that can be "read" from the culture and which corresponds to biblical revelation. It is the essence of incarnation that the truth of God in Christ be understood by a people through the vehicle of indigenous culture.

The one who witnesses, therefore, is to be a learner, a respectful inquirer of the culture. This is not something that can be done in a mechanical way. It is an attitude, an actual mode of living and interacting. Culture learning and the affirmation of people seeking to express Christ lifts up their dignity and promotes a will to believe. To urge indigenous leaders, together with members of the body, to look deeply into their own world-view and traditions for communication, worship, and witness honors both God and his people. This is the attitude that must characterize mission in our day (1989:25).

God did not endorse one culture to be sacred; rather, he uses every culture equally to communicate His message. God himself chose Hebrew culture in which to become incarnate, and used their language and frame of reference. Later he used Greek thought forms to communicate. The apostle Paul sought to be "all things to all men." He contextualized in order to avoid a cultural stumbling block or offense (*skandalon*). Later I will propose a "Trajectory Principle," one aim of which is dialogue with the given culture in order to make the culture a container of the Christian message.

Conn explains that the core idea of *skandalon* is not a matter of hurt feelings but of hindrance to Christian faith in Jesus Christ (1984:237). He proposes:

The theological apologetic of contextualization must be oriented toward this kind of offense. It must be ready to remove all unnecessary stumbling blocks that do not lie on the level of faith. And it must always insist on that particular element of Christianity that stands in direct conflict with the nonbeliever's mindset (1984:240).

McGavran articulated the idea simply: "Men like to become Christian without crossing racial, linguistic or class barriers" (1980:223). The Jerusalem Council set an example of this principle. The Apostles "did not constitute a definition of what was necessary for the salvation of the gentile Christians, but there was an attempt to solve the problem of a limited group of mixed communities where Jews and gentiles were living together" (J. Gresham Machen 1947:92). The Apostle James resolved the question:

It is my judgment, therefore, that we should not make it difficult for the gentiles who are turning to God. Instead we should write to them, telling them to abstain from food polluted by idols, from sexual immorality, from the meat of strangled animals and from blood. For Moses has been preached in every city from the earliest times and is read in the synagogues on every Sabbath (Acts 15:19–21).

James gave conditions only on issues that would have caused basic moral conflicts. The importance of this is seen in that even the Apostle Peter was carried away by problems with his own cultural protocol when he shunned eating with gentile Christians.

Culture is a neutral vehicle, like a container, whether it is used by God or by Satan. Don Richardson illustrates his idea by what he has termed a "redemptive analogy" by relating a Sawi cultural element, the "peace child," to God's eternal "Peace Child," Jesus (Richardson 1974).

God has always worked with people in the culture in which they are bound. Since God is not bound by any culture, he takes into account the total context in which people find themselves. If God uses human culture to communicate His message, we as his ambassadors, ought likewise to use the receptor's culture to convey the message. Schrieter forcefully asserts that without this cultural sensitivity we can expect "outside domination" or a "lapse into Docetism" (1985:21).

The contextual process requires that the communicators of the gospel begin with the receptor's context rather than their own. Dale Kietzman points out that the gospel must be "comprehensible entirely within the thought patterns and other bounds imposed by the pagan culture" (1974:126).

Unless communicators contextualize to forms of communication the people understand, the message will not be received. All communication involves symbols that link meanings with forms, persons, functions, and contexts (Hiebert 1985:142–143). This illustrates clearly the reason why Jesus was born in Hebrew culture, used their language and spoke in parables. It was that they might understand and change.

Contextualization assumes that God may use any symbol or form that has meaning in that context. Kraft remarks, "God in Jesus became so much a part of specific human context that many never even recognized that he had come from somewhere else" (1979:175). God obviously desires response from the receptors, and we share the same desire.

Characteristics of Contextualization

Several characteristics of contextualization become apparent in the process. It is done within the community and confession of faith; it is relevant, but not limited to, the situation at hand; and it is done to meet people's immediate needs as well as preparing them for Christ's second coming.

Communal—Confessional

Because conceptualization seeks to be obedient to Christ's demands upon His people and to meet their felt needs in their context, the starting point of contextualization is "from within the circle of faith-commitment," the believer's community (Nicholls 1979:55). Doing theology in context is a dialogue not only within the believing community but also with the surrounding cultural, socio-economic, political, religious, ecological, psychological, and demographic context.

It is an elaboration of confession and proclamation of loyalty to Christ Jesus from within the community of God to the surrounding world. It is the fulfillment of Jesus Christ's directive:

> "Go home to your family and tell them how much the Lord has done for you, and how he has had mercy on you." So the man went away and began to tell in the Decapolis how much Jesus had done for him. And all the people were amazed (Mk.5:19–20).

Korean immigrants, as a people group culturally distinct from their American leadership, must theologize together with their American leaders in order to convey the Christian message effectively to non-Christian Korean immigrants.

Confessionally, just as a person who has no personal relationship with Christ cannot adequately theologize, so also a believer isolated from the community of Christ cannot adequately theologize. This is sometimes a problem with theologians who do not have a living faith in Christ or do not theologize from within the community of faith. Confession is not only a matter of individuals' faith but that of the whole body of Christ. A.D.R. Polman puts it this way:

> To make confession is not a matter for one person alone but for the entire congregation of Christ. To the Church has been given the words of God, the entrusted charge and the oversight of doctrine built on the foundations of the apostles, prophets, the Church of the living God as the pillar and bulwark of the truth (Eph.2:20; 1 Tim.3:15) (1975:26).

Yet theologizing differs between the western and non-western worlds due to different communal dimensions. Differences should obviously be expected between the American and the Korean Church of the Nazarene in the U.S.A. Confessions and creeds are contextualized according to their particular historical place and time, yet as a community of believers (the church), we need to confess and struggle together. The Augsburg Confession was an official statement of the Lutheran position in the Roman Catholic dominated world of the 16th century, while the Westminster Confession was a Presbyterian confession in contrast to Anglican dominance. Contextualization is a communal determination to uphold the primacy and authority of scripture and a reaffirmation of faith in Christ Jesus, inviting those who do not have fellowship with Him to come (Mk.4:11; Col.4:5; 1 Thess.4:12). As Conn comments on such communities, "Their richest service lies in their function of translating the gospel to address the needs of their own day and cultural context" (1984:241). The 1982 Seoul Declaration reveals the communal struggles and agenda of contextualization for the future:

> Those of us in Asia will have to grapple with such questions as the resurgence of indigenous religions, the struggle for justice in the face of oppression, totalitarian ideologies and regimes, the tensions between traditional values, corruptions, and modern consumerism. To this end we need to develop our hermeneutical tools....

Those of us in Africa will have to take seriously the traditional African worldview, the reality of the spirit world, the competing ideologies, the resurgence of Islam and the contemporary cultural, religious and political struggles. Theology will have to explore ways of presenting the personal God and man. Also, it will seek to respond to the quest of human identity in the context of the dehumanizing history of colonial exploitation, tribal feuds and racial discrimination.

Those of us in Latin America will have to forge theology from within a context in which the social, economic and political structures are in a state of disarray, unable to close the gap between the rich and the poor and to solve the problems created by economics and technological dependence. Theology will have to give priority to problems relating to justice and peace, the control of the arms race, the evangelistic implications of demographic and urban church growth, the pathetic conditions of aboriginal people and other people groups, and the missiological challenge of popular religiosity and syncretism.

Together they draw the conclusion:

"With all our different emphases and varying cultures, we have experienced the reality of our oneness in Jesus Christ, of a theology in obedient service of our Lord Jesus Christ through the power of the Holy Spirit" (1983:10–12).

We see in each case how hermeneutical tools are different according to the context. The western hermeneutic for understanding is shaped by the sociological presuppositions of its dominant worldview.

The third world struggles with their theological identities, because their theology was imported from the West. It is self evident that in the theologizing process, the Korean Church of the Nazarene and American theologians must work together in a confession of faith in Christ relevant to our time.

Situational—Open Ended

Contextualization seeks to be situational. Nicholls addresses the matter of open-endedness: "Contextualizing of biblical theology in a changing world demands a rethinking of the whole process of doing theology" (1979:55). When cultural, social, political, and demographic transformations occur, theology must be flexible to change for the sake of the people.

The language is changed as well as the worship forms as one generation goes and a new generation comes. Biblical language was changed from Hebrew to Greek and Latin, just as the old King James Version is outdated for young people in this generation. The old hymnody, which was very contemporary generations ago, is now considered old fashioned by many and is often replaced by contemporary worship songs for the young generation.

Theology has been continually reformed for 2000 years of Christian history. We must not confuse canon with theology, but reform our theology to approach the Truth for continued relevance in every changing context. Therefore, open-endedness is necessary for propagating the gospel to every generation, every age, and every individual in history.

The trajectory model, which I shall propose, is constantly in motion to hit the target whatever its distance. The first generation of Korean immigrants is located differently from the American Nazarene, as is the second generation Nazarenes or Korean Nazarenes in Korea. The cultural and linguistic distances vary from the first generation, the 1.5 generation and the second generation. Therefore, the contextual model of gospel communication must be open ended to reach the target, the particular audience.

Existential—Prophetic

It is imperative for us to bear in mind that Jesus did not ignore the daily lives of people. Instead, he healed the sick, delivered people from demonic oppression, opened their ears, restored their sight, fed them, preached the good news, taught them, and provided points of contact for their conversion.

The goal of Christian communication is to reach the hearts of people so that they might receive a relevant, valid witness of Christ leading to repentance and salvation. If a theology is far from relating with daily felt needs, people will tend not to respond. To be existential, the gospel has not only to affirm the positive aspects of cultural values, but must also confront demonic and dehumanizing aspects of culture. God Himself promised, "He will not let your foot slip-he who watches over you will not slumber; indeed, he who watches over Israel will neither slumber nor sleep" (Ps.121:3–4).

Korean people go to the shaman or the fortuneteller to get help, protection, healing, and blessing. Is God or a theology not supposed to meet the Korean immigrants' daily felt needs for healing, deliverance, provision, and empowerment in this life? Few would be interested only in eternal life through Jesus Christ after they die.

While we preach the grace of Christ's first coming, we cannot ignore the judgment of His second coming. A complete gospel message must embrace both elements. But the prophetic criteria of theology are not limited to divine judgment. It also presents hope and grace from God through Jesus Christ, just as the prophets delivered divine oracles of judgment as well as hope and the grace of God. Prophetic criteria give a right perspective of life and redemption, as well as anticipating the Lord's second coming.

As we have dealt with contextualization in a general overview, we have seen how it has developed for two decades. We also have discussed the needs, criteria, and the characteristics of contextualization in order to lay some theoretical foundation for a proper contextualization for the Korean Church of the Nazarene in Southern California.

Ultimately my aim is to contextualize for the American Korean Church of the Nazarene, and for this I shall have to draw helpful aspects from among these models. But first we need to at look Korean culture to understand enough about its worldview to present a suitable contextual approach.

Chapter 4

KOREAN WORLDVIEW (A): SHAMANISM

The realm of shamanism is fundamental to Korean worldview. In approaching this subject, let us first look at worldview theory on a more general level.

General Worldview Theory

Worldview is a people's assumptions about the reality of their world and is studied through various dimensions. It is not only cross-cultural but also cross-disciplinary among various academic contexts, such as religion, anthropology, theology, and political science. The term "worldview" may denote different aspects: individual, corporate, personal, social, geographical (Oriental or Eastern), natural, supernatural, personal, impersonal, mechanic, or organic dimensions. While worldview has many facets, it is a universal phenomenon.

Scholars approach worldview with different explanations and various models. Michael Kearney defines it this way:

> The worldview of a people is their way of looking at reality. It consists of basic assumptions and images that provide a more or less coherent, though not necessarily accurate, way of thinking about world. A worldview compromises images of Self and of all

that is recognized as not-Self, plus ideas about relationships between them (1983:41).

Hiebert says, "The basic assumptions about reality which lie behind the beliefs and behavior of a culture are sometimes called worldview." Hiebert presents worldview assumptions as three dimensions of culture: the cognitive, the affective, and the evaluative. These dimensions underlie culture in largely implicit and unexampled ways (1985:45).

Robert Redfield clarifies worldview as being different from culture, ethos, mode of thought, and national character (1953:270). He defines the worldview of a people as "the way a people characteristically look outward upon the universe...." (1952:85).

Hiebert uses mechanic and organic analogies to analyze religious systems. By "mechanic analogies," living beings in a mechanistic system are manipulated by an impersonal force or formula and become subject to that mechanism—a very deterministic system. In the mechanistic view or mechanic analogy, both nature and humans can be controlled if the right formula is known. In a sense, we can become gods by controlling the power of destiny (1985:120).

The mechanistic concepts of *kismet* in Islam and *karma* in Hinduism parallel each other in many ways and both have parallels with magic and astrology. Just as the scientist uses formulas (impersonal, empirical forces) for his own benefit, the magician or astrologer controls supernatural forces by means of spells and charms. Such a view is amoral in character, since events are controlled by impersonal forces. Kraft describes this as "animatism" (1982:21,22).

By "organic analogy," Hiebert categorizes worldviews, which see the world in terms of living beings. Humans and nature (animals, plants, land, and water) are all assumed to have personalities and life (1987:14). Most non-western cultures see all the world as being alive with all elements relating to one another. This is also known as animism. Christianity fits the animistic category more than it does the mechanistic.

Figure 1
WORLDVIEW
(Adapted from Kraft 1986)

Functions of Explicit Systems

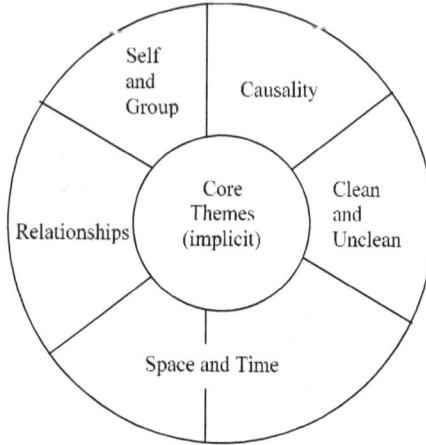

A culture's worldview is its central systematization of perception of reality. Thus, worldview is the system that explains reality. Disease is treated according to the culture's worldview. In a shamanistic worldview the cause of sickness is explained as a malevolent spirit. An America would say a virus or germ infection is the common sense explanation.

Figure 1 shows implicit and explicit structure of worldview and worldview themes.

Functions of Worldview

Worldview influences both the implicit meaning and explicit behavior of culture. Worldview is the "central control box" for five major functions integrated into the everyday life of people (Redfield quoted by Kraft 1979:53). These functions are: explanation, evaluation, psychological reinforcement, integration, and adaptation (Kraft 1979:54–57).

Worldview explains the way things are and how they got that way. Korean worldview explains, through the *Dangun Myth*, how the nation of Korea came to exist. Every Korean custom and tradition has a story to explain it. When Koreans dream of deceased parents or grandparents, the dream explains and communicates something to the dreamer. Korean folklore, riddles, songs, maxims, mask dances, games, and legends, are replete with stories of explanation.

Many Korean legends, for example, concern the filial piety of a son or daughter and the loyalty of a wife. *Simchung chun* is a story about a damsel who sacrificed herself as a donation to Buddha in order to bring her blind father's sight back. The intent of this story is to admonish young people to be dutiful sons and daughters and good Buddhists.

Besides explaining how things are, worldview *evaluates* whether things are right or wrong, good or bad, pleasing or displeasing. Value systems are closely related to explanations. As part of worldview assumptions, value systems give meaning, sanctions and judgment to the social group in its educational, political, social, communicational and economic structures.

Worldview provides *psychological reinforcement* in times of crisis. There are various rituals and ceremonies to enable people to cope with crises of birth, death, illness, drought and natural disaster as well as the transitions of puberty, marriage, planting, the new year, and harvest (Kraft 1979:55). For example, in time of drought in a Korean farming village, the farmers will hold a ceremony to the dragon god for rain.

Worldview provides security and supports the people as it is the foundation of behavioral patterns and ceremonies. It also integrates the elements in the cultural system. When a new idea is introduced, the worldview perceives, filters, conceptualizes, and validates it for the sake of systematization.

R.M. Keesing and F.M. Keesing note that a peoples' worldview "establishes and validates basic premises about the world and man's place in it; it relates the strivings and emotions of men to them" (1971:303).

When President Jung Hee Park introduced the new idea of reformation through the "New Village Movement" to revitalize the nation, he worked hard not only to change the visible social and economic systems, but also to literally alter people's thinking their very worldview. The government executed the new policy through ideas, beliefs, songs, themes, concepts, and systems by broadcasting, teaching, publishing, and campaigning. The whole nation began to believe the new idea and began to cooperate with the new movement. Attention to the people's worldview enabled the ideas and practices of this reformation to be integrated into the existing culture.

Worldview *integrates* and sanctions the function of values, goals, and institutions. In Korean culture, filial piety to parents is among the most important ethical codes as well as one of the most highly regarded norms of society. In a Korean home the mother-in-law has power over the daughter-in-law, even to intervene in her marriage and rule her kitchen.

In Korean public transportation it is considered rude if a young person does not give a seat to a standing senior citizen. Since the status of man is higher than that of woman in Korean thinking, a Korean wife walks three steps behind her husband. Many a wife will carry the baby on her back and a diaper bag or whatever else in her hands while the man walks unencumbered without feeling guilt or shame. Their worldview affirms that these mores are normal and appropriate.

Worldview provides a way of *adaptation* when change besets a culture or person. Under the pressure of rapid change, a culture easily disintegrates. The adaptational nature of worldview reduces "internal structural contradiction" in the process of cultural change by adjusting people's perception of reality (Wallace 1966:27). If a society faces ideological difficulty, Wallace notes that "it may be easier to reinterpret values than to reorganize the society" (1966:29).

The function of adaptation leads a person replace one idea with another. Adaptation endows an ability to reconcile the differences or contradictions from the old ideas into the new ones when done with respect and modification the result is replacement (revitalization) (Kraft 1979:57). Worldview helps a culture or individual undergoing change to lessen the cultural distortion or disequilibrium and leads to adjustment and replacement.

In the following chapter I will discuss major themes of Korean and American worldviews. I consider differences between the two to be the major cause of gaps in communication of the Christian message.

Korean worldview cannot be understood apart from the history of Shamanism, Buddhism, Confucianism, and more recently, Christianity. The three dimensions of Korean worldview before the introduction of Christianity can be categorized into both mechanic and organic elements.

Organically, Koreans are deeply saturated in a syncretistic mix of Shamanism, Buddhism, and Confucianism. I will review and analyze Shamanism, Buddhism, and Confucianism prior to the introduction of Christianity to discover how all have influenced Korean worldview. This will shed light on the analyses of each in terms of organic and mechanic, as well as this-worldly and otherworldly elements. I will examine how these pre-Christian Korean religions met the felt needs of people at the worldview level. Also I will select major worldview themes developed in the individual Korean mind and in the social structure.

Korean Worldview

Of the three major influences on Korean worldview, let us look first at shamanism, then the initiation of mudang, and finally *Yeoldu Kori*, the Twelve Rites.

The Shamanistic Dimension

Shamanism in Korea has been integrated into Korean life for five thousand years, penetrating Korean minds and interplaying with Buddhism and Confucianism in every integral aspect of their cultural patterns and behaviors. According to the Dangun Myth, which is the account of Korean national foundation, the first king, Dangun, was also the first shaman and priest figure of his nation who offered sacrifice on behalf of the nation.

Thus we begin with the Shamanistic dimension discussing the identity, function and work of a shaman.

Identity of the Shaman. In the Encyclopedia of Religion John Arnott MacCulloch defines shamanism as "a primitive religion of Polytheism or polydemonism with strong roots in nature worship, and generally with a supreme god over all" (1958:441). Mircea Eliade defines today's shamanism as "a religious phenomenon of Siberia and Central Asia, from the Tungusic word 'saman'" (1964:4). He adds, "Any ecstatic cannot be considered a shaman; the shaman specializes in a trance during which his soul is believed to leave his body and ascend to the sky or descend to the underworld" (1964:5).

This concept of shaman holds for Paraguayan Guarani shamen. These ancient shamen made their bodies light by jolts, jumps and constant dancing until they could fly. Shamen have religious and spiritual power and authority to infer in administration and justice (cf. Cadogan 1962:48–49, and Metraux 1928:69–94). However, Korean shamen do not fast and pray or fly. Eliade mainly dealt with the trance type ecstasy phenomenon of shamanism.

There are some distinctions between the *mudang* (Korean shaman) and Eliade's shaman. The *mudang* are initiated by a god's descent or by possession of the *mudang* spirit, while other shamen are initiated in different, yet related in ways. Shamanism is in fact a universal religious phenomenon including magicians, sorcerers, and mediums who mediate between gods, spirits and people.

As mediums, the Korean *mudang* have spiritual power to bridge the spiritual world and natural world. They seek to "control the fate of man by influencing the spirit through direct contact" (Tong-shik Ryu 1973:64). Since ancient Koreans believed in many gods, the mudang mediated between men and the various Korean gods, performing rites to connect the natural and spiritual worlds.

The Pantheon of Shamanism. Shamanism includes a plethora of gods and spirits, connecting the spiritual and natural worlds.

"Hananim," in Korean shamanism, is the supreme god, also known as, "Okwhangsanche" (Yellowjade Heavenly God). From ancient times, Koreans believed in the supreme being Hananim. Hananim is not related to creation or salvation. Rather, it is the highest spirit or god; beneath it are all other spirits, including mountain, water, earth, and wind (Sang-Hee Moon 1982:28).

Hananim is called upon for rain, and Korean women call Hananim in front of a white ceramic bowl of water in the kitchen or any sacred place. Homer Hulbert observes correctly that Koreans consider Hananim to be the supreme ruler of the universe (1969:404).[1]

Sin (pronounced "sheen") and *kwisin* are the two general types of spirits. *Sin* are supposed to be benevolent while *kwisin* are malevolent. All the rituals by family shaman, housewives, or professional shaman who specialize in numerous cleansing rituals are directed at *sin* and *kwisin*.

Non-human *kwisin* are called *kwisin* or *dokkabi*. They are thought to reside in cemeteries, wilderness, caves, empty houses, funeral palanquins, forests, valleys, gloomy and dark places, or old castles.

There are different kinds of *kwisin,* which roam around causing trouble and sickness. In the shamanistic world, human sickness is caused by a *kwisin's* entering the body or catching a person. All mental illnesses, as well as traffic accidents, are caused by *kwisin*. Colds, malaria, typhoid, measles and cholera are all thought to be the result of different types of *kwisin*.

Spirits of the dead can also be called *kwisin*. Examples include those who die prematurely, die by an enemy's hand, die in an improper place on the street, die in another city, die by drowning, or die as a bachelor, virgin, or beggar. A *kwisin* may cause injury or sickness to surviving relatives. Not all such souls become *kwisin;* it depends on how a person dies. It is important to die after being married, at home, or in a natural way to avoid becoming a *kwisin* after death. *Jinogui kut* and *haewon kut* are rites to comfort the *kwisin* or to chase them away.[2]

There are several categories in a general pantheon, including water, mountain, earth, and trees that are mentioned below.

Obang Changgun (Five-point Generals) are the major spirits which are supposed to rule north, east, south, west, and the center of heaven. They are vigorously worshipped and cajoled by blind males and soothsayers, the *pansu*. A *pansu* is accompanied by a *shinchang* spirit, a lieutenant under *obang changgun*.

Tojisin (Gods of Earth) are earth spirits who are lords of rice or barley fields, and gods of the house or any location. Before burial takes place a person's gravesite must be cleansed, and sacrifices offered to the god of the earth. When people go on a picnic dinner, everyone throws the first spoonful of food to appease the spirit of the area out of fear of the spirit.

Sansin (Mountain Gods) appear as old men with white hair, beards and white cloaks. In this mountainous country, from the time of ancient Korean mythology, mountains have always been sacred. *Sansin* appear in pictures riding tigers' backs. In any

Korean Buddhist temple there is a shrine of a mountain god, an example of how Buddhism has synthesized with shamanism.[3]

Sungwhangdang (village or mountain pass god's shrine) is the name of an altar on a hill or mountain pass surrounded by small rocks and pebbles. A passerby makes a wish and throws a stone for a safe trip. Some people hang on the altarpieces of clothes as a fetish. Also, professional shaman and lay people make their sacrifices and petitions to the spirit (Shearer 1966:22).

Yongsin or *yuwang* (water spirit or dragon) are gods of the water. If someone travels by boat, the housewife goes to a well to sacrifice and pray as priest of the household. This spirit is the lord of water in any form, including river, stream, well, lake, or ocean. This spirit supposedly resides in bottomless lakes and ponds. It is worshipped by casting food into the waters and offering prayers, particularly in early January. In time of drought, it is petitioned for rain (C. Clark 1928:203).

Trees are thought to be divine or inhabited by spirits and are worshipped. Peach trees have power to drive away *kwisin*. The ginkgo tree and cedar tree have resident spirits, and large elm trees are usually worshipped (C. Clark 1929:207).

House Pantheons appear in every traditional home. Worshipping *chosangsin* (ancestral spirits of the dead) is thought to bring prosperity to the descendants. Within the house pantheon is the *sungjusin*, lord of the house. It has a fetish on the beam of the ceiling above the living room. When people move they take this fetish to the new house because of the belief that the *sungjusin* resides in it. *Chesukbulsa*, borrowed from Buddhism, is the god of longevity and welfare for the children of the house (Yunsik Chang 1982:31). *Chuwangsin* is the god of the kitchen and is enshrined in a bowl full of water. *Samsin* is the god of fertility. Thought to be three gods, *samsin* is enshrined in three bowls of rice and water in front of a newborn baby. *Tojusin* is the god of the house site and is the god of treasure of the house. It is enshrined in a jar covered with a bundle of rice straw. There are also gods of the gate and lavatory. Every fall, each god is offered a sacrifice of a rice cake as a thanksgiving offering. Sometimes a shaman is invited and performs these rituals.

Types of Shamen. There are both professional and family shamen. Professional shamen perform rites as their occupation, while family shamen are housewives who conduct simple shamanistic practices at home (Chang 1982:38–40). Professional shamen are of three types: inherited, spirit appointed, and spirit trained.

Hereditary shamen and spirit-appointed shamen have religious experiences and communicate with spirits. The trained shamen are more mechanical and can at best predict the future by divination. A hereditary shaman is good at singing and dancing; spirit appointed shamen are known as prophetic shamen.

The functions of shamen are: priestly (mediator between people and gods), prophetic (predicting destiny and fortune), clinical (healing the sick and expelling evil spirits), and recreational (entertain by singing and dancing). Charismatic prophetic shamen are the most traditional and most in demand. Yet, all are in the business of bridging the gap between this world and the spirit world for the sake of protection, security, and fortune.

Mudang is the name for a female shaman. *Paksu* is a male shaman. *Mudang* and *paksu* both seek to control the fate of man by influencing the spirits through direct contact. This is done through performing *kut*. According to Ryu, *kut* is "the cultural expression of the aboriginal world of 'oneness'" (1973:14). It is a shamanistic séance "in which gods and man have a direct dialogue, and the sacred and profane coexist" (1973:13).

A *kut* is a ritual held by a *mudang* for purposes such as healing, invoking fortunes, exorcising demons, preventing disasters, blessing the family, and foretelling the future.

Pansu is a blind *paksu*. *Yubok* is a blind *mudang*. Both use the mantra as well as assistance from the *shinchang* spirits (Clark 1929:180–188). *Mudang* and *pansu* are spirit possessed, charismatic shamen and specialize in rituals of *kut*. *Pansu* and *yubok* are diviners and use a book of incantations. Fortune telling is the chief function of *pansu*.

The Chinese characters for *pan* ("discern") and *su* ("destiny") are best translated "decider of fate or destiny" (Horace Underwood 1908:93). *Yubok* are rare, and because they are simple diviners, they are held in low social status.

Pansu have the important function of expelling evil spirits that cause sickness, insanity, disaster or bad luck by the help of *obang sinchang*, the generals of the four directions north, east, south, and west, and the center of heaven. *Pansu* and *mudang* often work together. *Pansu* use mechanical forces of incantations of books, charms, and talisman.

Mudang communicate, cajole, and appease these spirits by means of bribery while *pansu* use coercion. *Pansu* use books of incantations, which are called *kyung*, and spells. The most commonly used book is *Okju Kyung* ("the Jade Book").

This book deals with the supreme being called "Chunjon" (Hananim), the Shaker of the Nine Heavens and the "myriads of his minions." Incantations of the book are supposed to heal fevers, twenty-five types of stomach worms, and countless bodily infirmities.

The Jade Book also claims an extravagant power of healing and immunity from pestilence: even if a whole village is being swept by a plague, the book offers a cure. It promises protection from thieves, robbers, wolves and even drought. Reciting this book is also supposed to bring rain. This book further claims to cure various diseases from tuberculosis to cancer. Charles Clark considers *The Jade Book* to be the "Bible of Shamanism" (1929:188).

The *pansu* nevertheless uses a variety of books of spells and incantations to invoke and coerce spirits by the mechanical forces contained in the books; therefore, they are often called "incanters" Whereas shamans use the spirits, *pansu* use the mechanical forces contained in the books of incantations.

Jikwan (Geomancers) and *ilkwan* (Lucky Day Selectors) are also types of shamen. Geomancy (*pungsujiri*) is widely known and practiced in Korean folk life. It is a pseudo-scientific system of water and wind theory introduced from China. A geomancer uses this theory in order to select sites for houses, temples, buildings and graces. Charles Clark explains geomancy as the "science of water and wind," the work of selecting propitious sites for residences and other buildings, and most importantly for burial sites (1929:189).

The most propitious sites, called *myungdang*, are supposed to cause prosperity and even acquisition of a higher place in the royal court. The deeply symbolic principle of *jachungryong* "a blue dragon on the left" and *wubaekho* "a white tiger on the right" is the major principle of geomancy by which a *myundang* is measured. Furthermore, every type of landscape is described by the four mechanical forces of geomancy: decay, prosperity, right, and wrong.

These elements are thought to influence the destinies of people. Therefore, it was the highest expression of filial piety to select the finest burial sites for one's ancestors because the ancestral spirits were thought to reside in their gravesites. Accordingly, geomancers have been, and continue to be, much in demand. Nationally renowned geomancers were called to decide the location for royal palaces, the capital city, and even today, graveyards.

Geomancy is rooted in divination from *The Book of Change* combined with the principle of the great ultimate, yin/yang, and the five agencies, wood, fire, metal, water and earth (See Jung Young Lee 1982:6–24). Charles Clark quotes Martin's definition of geomancy as a "debased offshoot of a degenerate Taoism" (1929:188). Charles Clark records the relationship between *chikwan* and *mudang* in working together:

> All sites had their guardian spirits, the earth gods, and gods of the mountains, and the Chikwan needed to cultivate them in order to be successful in his business. When the earth was broken in the digging of the grave, he must be capable of so directing matters that the spirits of the soil would not be outraged too much and themselves bring about disaster. The actual exorcising away of any spirits in the soil just before the body was laid to rest was usually the work of Mootangs [*mudang*] or done under their direction, but preparations for it were made by the Chikwan (1929:189–190).

The earliest historical records of geomancy are from the Silla period. The founder of Silla, Dal-hae Suk, made use of geomancy to select the ground on which to build his home on Yansan Mountain (Chong-hong Park 1975:130–131). Chi-Yon Chae predicted the fall of Silla and the rise of the Koryo dynasty.

Geomancy was often used in political maneuvering. It became synthesized with Buddhism, with monks being involved in geomancy. In the beginning of the Yi dynasty the Buddhist monk Muhak, also a powerful geomancer, predicted the 500 years' reign and downfall of the Yi dynasty. He based his prediction on the geomantic site of the capital, Seoul.

Due to Confucian teaching of filial piety, non-Christian Koreans still believe in the mechanical forces of sites; therefore they make every effort to find *myundang* to bury their dead, which will bring prosperity and success to the offspring. Consistent with geomancy there is a mystic belief in the relationship between person's character and the mountain range of his birthplace. The belief explains how the lineage of the famous characters are influenced by the spirits of a famous mountain range. According to geomantic explanation, every Korean president was influenced by the mountain range where he was born.

The following article is a geomantic explanation about the place of origin of former president Doowhan Chun:

> Some twelve kilometers southeast of Hapchon, Kyunsang Namdo, lies this small village of 87 houses at the foot of Mt. Youngduk, (dragon virtue?), a branch of Mt. Sobaek (the massive mountain whose range divides southern Korea into eastern and western macro-regions). The River Hwang... runs south through Hapchon for some distance. However, the river suddenly runs backward to run north for 6 kilometers and regains its original course near the village, drawing the contour of a dragon. Just beyond the village is a pond, which never runs dry during the worst drought. Ancients would say the hamlet would produce a great man some day (Korea Herald quoted in Griffin Dix 1982:56).

Today many non-Christian Koreans believe in geomancy. Even Korea's mass media uses geomancers. Because of geomancy, people often exhume ancestors, relocating them to better sites—a practice thought to relieve offspring of affliction by unhappy ancestral spirits buried in undesirable places. The geomancer is called to find new gravesites to bring a solution to the problems.

Ilkwan select the "lucky day" for kut, weddings, business openings, moving, of funerals. During the dynasties a king was told by the *ilkwan* when to take a trip or to go to have conjugal relations, according to the principle of the five elements and of yin/yang theory. The *ilkwan* knows uses the formulae of mechanic forces of the *juyeok chaek*, a debased offshoot of *The Book of Change*. Selecting a proper day for events (*taek il,* "receiving the date") is essential for major events, especially rites of passage in Koreans' minds (Clark 1929:190–191).

Cheom refers to divination. When unpredicted troubles come upon the family or business, some friend will advise the person who has the problem, "*Cheom chireo kabayo*" ("Go and see the fortune teller!"). A fortuneteller is called *cheomjaengi*. However, in precise language, *cheomgaengi* refers to those who divine by interpreting omens, portents, and signs of the spirit world. *Cheomjaengi* is difficult to define, as Barbara Young describes, "Not exactly shamans, not quite priests, not really astrologers, and not licensed psychotherapists, the women who earn their living telling fortunes in Korea's cities offer advice, insights, and interpretations to a kaleidoscope of clientele" (1983:121).

Cheomjaengi who use the *Sajuchaeck* (a divination book using the "four pillars" of birth date, hour, month, and year) follow mechanical formulae and forces. Most *cheomjaengi* divine by reading rice, throwing coins or using birds. They are socially marginal, despised and outcast people. Yet they manipulate lives and assist people in times of disaster, trouble and sorrow simply by telling their fortunes or fates.

Many people use palm reading, facial bone reading, or birth dates (hour, day, month, year) for divination. The five elements of fire, water, wood, iron, and earth interact among people according to birthday hour, month, and year. Some people use a modern, distorted Book of Change to predict their life destiny.

The Initiation of Mudang. An initiatory illness called *mubyung* is required to be a *mudang*. Jong Il Kim points out the initiatory illness of a spirit appointed *mudang* as "a religious phenomenon that involves a severe physical illness, dream of the spirits, and the ecstasy experiences" (1985:82). Eliade concludes that it "cannot be a mere sickness because of the mudang's knowledge of the mechanism behind illness" (Eliade 1964:31). Jong Il Kim thinks *mubyung* should be considered a religious phenomenon rather than the mental disorder it appears to be (1985:83).

According to Tae-gon Kim's research, the initiation illness involves: (1) a loss of appetite for food and emaciation, (2) a light-headed feeling of flightiness and suffocation, (3) an excited, unstable and crazy feeling (1972:21). When the illness is known, an established mudang comes and holds an initiation rite. The established mudang then becomes a mother mudang and trains this novice mudang.

The Work of Mudang. It is the fundamental nature of shamanism to perceive all human problems, including life and death, calamity, and happiness as being from supernatural causes rather than the individual's intrapsychic cause. In this worldview (or cultural context) the causes of diseases, calamity and happiness are caused by spirits, gods, and evil spirits. It is natural for the mudang to be called to solve problems, to cure, to chase away evil spirits, give guidance, and bless by cajoling, appeasing, propitiating, and coercing spirits.

The mudang performs pudak kori, a simple rite for healing by offering food and prayer for the sick, in the case of ancestral spirits' getting upset or intrusion of kwisin. If it is a serious case of illness, mudang and pansu work together to chase away kwisin, and in a process called byung kut (Ryu 1973:16).[4] The word, pudak kori (the rites of casting out demons and healing the sick) has been secularized in daily use: when things are not going well, people will express habitually, "We need pudak kori for that." It has simply become an expression of distress.

A mudang performs a kut for good yearly crop harvest or for the construction of a new building. Sacrifices are made to ensure blessings.[5] Even Korean Air holds a kut before the first flight of a new aircraft. This kut is called kibokche or jaesu kut. A blessing of longevity is chesuk kut (Ryu 1973:16). To pray for the blessing for the children is samsin puri and for the peace of the house is sungjumagi. For expelling evil spirits, pansu and yubok use incantations of the book, Eumpookyung, to invoke the shinchang spirits to drive out evil spirits. Mudang cajole and drive out evil spirits by bribing them.

A mudang is believed able to prolong life. "Myung dari Gulda" ("Hang up the bridge of life") is the phrase expressing how Korean mothers sell their children to gods through mudang. As a result, these gods or spirits are thought to prolong the children's lives—all a result of a mudang's prayer. My brother Sung Dae, who is now a pastor, was sold to seven different mudang, called "step mother," for long life. This was my mother's response to the high infant mortality rate at that time. The mudang takes responsibility to pray for the child's protection and long life.

Dano kut (see Ryu 1973:15) and pyulsin kut (see Tong-Gwon Im 1973:5–9) are examples of communal rites of festivity conducted by shaman to harmonize the spirits of a village community into "oneness." Throughout history in times of drought, Korean kings have always invited shamen to hold rites for invocation of rain (Moon 1982:20). When the mudang dance and chant myths, people are entertained and pleased to watch them.

As mentioned earlier, kut is a prayer ceremony invoking different spirits for blessing, good luck, protection, healing and well-being to the family sponsoring the kut. Ryu elaborates:

> "Kut" is the regeneration of the aboriginal world of oneness, in which man not only had dialogue with the deities directly without any gulf, but also was sublimated into divinity and merged into the god to be united as one with him. The climax of "Kut" is the trance in which ecstasy is experienced when the words of the "Mudang" become the divine sayings. So the "kut" is concluded with hearing of divine words of blessings, that is receiving oracles (1973:14).

The sequenced rites of a *kut* ceremony develop its meaning and its purpose. Generally *mudang* are possessed by the spirits they invoke in their *kut*. *Jaesu kut* is a ritual for elimination of bad fortune and invocation of good fortune. According to Tae-Gon Kim the sequence of the *Jaesu kut* involves twelve rites (1978:43). In Figure 2 I have categorized the twelve rites with their corresponding shamanistic acts and costumes.

Figure 2
TWELVE SHAMANISTIC RITES

Name of the Rite	Shamanistic Act	Shaman's Dress
1. Pujong Kori	Chasing the devil	Everyday clothes
2. Kamang Kori	Responding to gods	Military overcoat
3. Malmyong Kori	Blessing for souls of ancestors	General's deep blue shirt
4. Sangsan Kori	The god of the high mountain	General's blue shirt, overcoat, combat uniform
5. Pyulsang Kori	The god of smallpox	General's skirts and combat uniform
6. Taegam Kori	High ranking officials	Combat uniform and felt hat
7. Chesok Kori	Buddhist chesok deity	White chansam over hogu skirt
8. Hogu Kori	For food	Hogu skirt
9. Songju Kori	The god of residences	Red military uniform and Korean hat
10. Kunnung Kori	Military heroes	Red military uniform and Korean hat
11. Changbu Kori	For actors	Changbu's clothes
12. Twitchon Kori	Last act	Everyday clothes

Explanation of the Twelve Rites (Yeoldu Kori). These twelve rites are the basic rites for *kut* in general. The rites of kut reveal Korean felt needs to which Christians can respond in conceptualized ways. *Kuts* for different purposes follow the same basic steps.

The Purpose of Rituals

In the rituals of a kut, there are structured inner principles to be followed. The introductory prayers invoke the spirits to separate the sacred and profane worlds. Other prayers offer expulsion of spirits, and blessings. Following the shamanistic rites is my modification of Ryu's inner structures of kut.

Figure 3
INNER STRUCTURES OF *KUT*

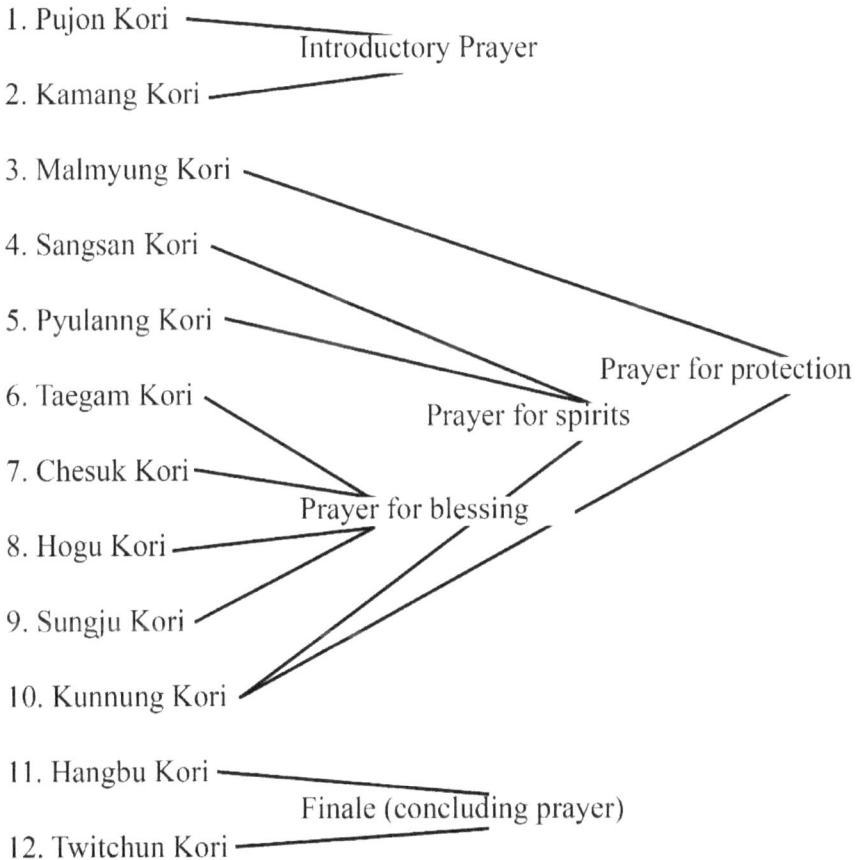

1. Pujon Kori
2. Kamang Kori

Introductory Prayer

3. Malmyung Kori
4. Sangsan Kori
5. Pyulanng Kori
6. Taegam Kori

Prayer for protection

Prayer for spirits

7. Chesuk Kori

Prayer for blessing

8. Hogu Kori
9. Sungju Kori
10. Kunnung Kori

11. Hangbu Kori

Finale (concluding prayer)

12. Twitchun Kori

Ryu sums up the meaning and the purpose of the rituals:

> The core elements of the "kut" lie in the communion between gods and man. In their belief, it is not man or nature that rules over all things of the world, life and death, as well as fortunes and misfortunes of man; but it is entirely providence and the acts of gods. Accordingly, in order to control the world of nature or man's destiny one ought to have the right fellowship with gods who are the source of power and let them control all these things as one wishes. Therefore...the "Mudang" invites gods, entertains them and listens to their will or oracles and obeys them (1973:16).

Summary

Shamanism is a pragmatic belief system for people in this-worldly life to seek fortune and avoid misfortune. It is thoroughly existential. Malevolent and benevolent spirits are carefully distinguished, and every human problem of evil and good is explained by gods or spirits. The world is seen as being alive. Yet there is no attempt to explain anything beyond this world. There are no concepts of sin, life, or death. Shamanism is an explanation system for problems of life and death, sickness, disaster, calamities, failure, and misfortunes in this world only.

Shamanism is deeply pervasive throughout Korean folk culture. Because of its basic existential nature, it has met the felt needs of folk life in a way Confucianism and Buddhism could not. Shamanism is deeply rooted, without governmental or institutional propagation or support. Indeed these groups often suppressed and persecuted shamanism. Though it had been suppressed and persecuted at the surface level, shamanism is still deeply rooted in people's minds after 5000 years of history.

Chapter 5

KOREAN WORLDVIEW (B): BUDDHISM, CONFUCIANISM AND CHRISTIANITY

With shamanism as the basic underlying folk religion of Korea, Buddhism was imported and later flourished as a state religion. Upon the collapse of Buddhism, Confucianism was introduced, and like Buddhism before it, Confucianism synthesized with shamanism. As Confucianism failed to meet people's needs, Koreans grew open to receiving Christianity.

The Buddhistic Dimension

Buddhism influenced Korean worldview through three major time periods and laid down several themes fundamental to Korean worldview.

The Three Kingdom Period (ca. 57 B.C.– 668 A.D.)

The Korean people have believed and worshipped Hananim, "heavenly god," as the supreme god who has mercy and charity, and helps people. Hananim punishes the bad and helps the good. Therefore, Koreans rebuke a wicked person saying, "Aren't you afraid of Hananim?" From generation to generation mothers and grandmothers pleaded to Hananim, rubbing their palms together in front of a bowl full of water in the kitchen or some other sacred place in the home. Virtually without any doctrinal foundation, the concept of Hananim existed in the Koreans' minds.

Doctrine. Buddhism was introduced to the three Kingdoms, offering a new cosmology, salvation, worldly life conduct, central value of Karma or causality, *Ahimsa*, and the Great Enlightenment, which Buddha had entered into.

To Buddha, individuals could become omnipotent and omniscient through the process of self-realization. Anyone can become a Buddha, one who is equal to a god in nature. Buddhism considers supernatural powers to be intrinsic to human nature. Through systematic methods of self-realization, supernatural potential is cultivated and utilized. These methods include celibacy, fasting, meditation, prayers, and chanting.

The idea of "karma," the cosmic forces of cause and effect, explains present conditions as being a result of past causes. The concept of karma fostered the Korean concept of fate, *palcha,* by infiltrating the *Book of Change's yin* and *yang* theory. Both karma and *yin/yang* are mechanistic principles to explain or direct blame in times of misfortune.

Ahimsa (non-violence) is another fundamental Buddhist precept in which no living thing should be killed (Sung-Bae Park 1982:72). Vegetarianism and a monastic lifestyle were natural offshoots of ahimsa, especially as it mixed with karma. Some devout Buddhist kings prohibited hunting or killing any animals. Thus, Buddhism led to other-worldly asceticism.

Monasticism. To achieve the "Great Enlightenment" and ascetic self-discipline, many people renounced secular life and entered monasteries. Consequently, monasticism became prominent, and monasteries emerged as the center of elite education for the nation (Sung-Bae Park 1982:72–73). The monks in monasteries practiced fasting, meditation, vegetarianism, and celibacy, as well as chanting mantras. Monasticism represented an effort to set up an ideal world by renouncing the secular world. Salvation would come as the monastic order expanded to replace secular society, including the state. This idealistic other-worldly religion was doomed to conflict with the this-worldly concerns of secular, political order. Nevertheless, many temples, shrines, towers, and images of Buddha were erected from the time of the three kingdoms to the Koryo Kingdom's downfall at the turn of 15th century.

Koguryo Kingdom. According to The Chronicle of the Three Kingdoms, Buddhism was introduced into Korea in 372 A.D. during the second year of King Sosurim of Koguryo. In 393 A.D. King Sosurim became a devout Buddhist and ordered his people to follow Buddha. He later erected nine temples in Pyongyang. This fused Buddhism with the state and allowed Buddhism to influence political, social and religious structures (Moon 1974:15). Soon the ruling class was largely Buddhist. Monks functioned as religious leaders, doctors, architects, educators, and lawyers. This wedding of Buddhism to the state strongly influenced peoples' beliefs. Buddhism synthesized with the accepted traditional religion, shamanism. The surface religion was Buddhism, but at the deep level of people's practice it was distorted as shamanized Buddhism. Ultimately, the result was a secularization and corruption of Buddhism.

Paekche Kingdom. In 384 A.D. an Indian monk, Maranata, brought Buddhism to Paekche in the reign of King Chimnu. He was welcomed and lived in the palace. One year later the king built a temple at the capital and appointed 12 monks (Clarence Weems 1962:66). "In 599 A.D. King Pob passed a law forbidding the killing of animals for food" and erected Wanghungsa temple, appointing thirty monks. Also King Song sent missionaries to Japan with books and images, urging the Japanese to adopt Buddhism (Moon 1974:16).

Silla Kingdom. The Silla Kingdom received Buddhism in 426 A.D. Initially resistance was strong, yet eventually Buddhism flourished more here than in the other two kingdoms. An Indian, "Mong Mukhoja," came to Silla when King Nullji ruled and ventured to evangelize, but failed due to strong opposition by traditional Shamanism In 528 A.D. because of the death of martyr Ichadon, King Pophung converted and proclaimed Buddhism the official religion of the land. He prohibited the killing of all living animals and ordered fishing and hunting equipment destroyed. In 544 A.D. King Chinhung built Hyoryungsa and many monasteries. Later Chinhung himself became a monk. Notably, "Buddha was venerated as the protector of the country rather than the savior of the people" (Moon 1974:16).

Unified Silla Period (668–935 A.D.)

After Silla defeated Paekche (660 A.D.) and Koguryo (668 A.D.) it established a unified kingdom. For the first time Silla established a unified kingdom throughout the land of Korea (57 B.C.–935 A.D.). It was during this time that Buddhism reached its peak and dominated the nation. Several of the most famous Buddhist temples were built around the prefecture of the capital, and most remain today. During the unified Silla period numerous Buddhist sects were introduced. But two sects most impacted the common people: they were Hinayana, which developed *Son* (or Zen) Buddhism, and Mahayana, called *Chongtojong* (Pure Land). The *Son* sect emphasizes meditation (the very word *Son* translates "meditation"). The Pure Land sect taught that one could obtain salvation (the Pure Land) by praying to the Bodhisattva spirit. This sect appealed to the grass root population and became the largest sect in Unified Silla (Moon 1974:18).

In Pure Land Buddhism no grasp of doctrines or scriptural knowledge of Buddhist sutras was requested; merely chanting "Nammu Amitabul" was enough to invoke the name of the Buddha and profess one's faith in Amita Buddha. Pure Land Buddhism appealed to the masses precisely because it gave hope to those who were burdened and suffering. Pure Land Buddhism did not give comfort in this world but instead preached rebirth into the paradise of the next world.

Koryo Period (918¬–1392 A.D.)

The founder of the Koryo Kingdom, Wanggun, was a devout Buddhist. He built several temples at the inauguration of the Kingdom, dedicating it to Buddha. "His policy of reverence for Buddhism was carried out throughout the Koryo Dynasty" (Moon 1974:18). The golden age of Buddhism reached the zenith of its power during the Koryo Kingdom, when it again became the state religion and monks mentored the state. A priest could reach a rank of instructor of the nation (kuksa) in the hierarchy as a spiritual mentor to the king. In fact, the king himself bowed before his instructor (Hei Chu Kim 1982:88). Buddhism, as an idealistic religion was doomed to conflict with the political structure. While Buddhism in theory renounced the world, its adherents were deeply involved in socio-politico-economic power structures. This power play led to the corruption of Buddhism, and, due to its interwovenness with the state, consequently led to the downfall of the entire Koryo Dynasty.

Yi Dynasty (1392–1909 A.D.)

The Yi Dynasty saw to the destruction of the previous kingdom and began to pressure Buddhism and its temples intensely until Buddhism disappeared from the surface level of power structures (Cf. Hei Chu Kim 1982:89). Buddhism was submerged under the folk level and was secretly being married to shamanism and Taoism in folk religions, because the new regime did not allow Buddhists to reexamine and reinterpret their religious ideology in the face of the new context. The masses were not able to comprehend the doctrines of karma and salvation; they only venerated the stone images of the Bosal, Buddha, and the towers, shrines, and temples to procure blessing and power for their problems. The *Sutras* were inaccessible to the masses because of their inscrutability and complexity. Therefore, on the folk level the other-worldly religion was bound to shift toward a this-worldly religion.

Summary of the Buddhistic Dimension

After Buddhism was imported to Korea during the Three Kingdom Period. Buddhistic culture and the ethos of the nation began to blossom. At first Buddhism suffered, but later it became the state religion of the Three Kingdom Period. Indeed, Buddhism became the state religion of unified Silla Kingdom and Koryo Kingdom for about 1500 years of Korean history. Since Buddhism overpowered the socio-politic-economic system of the state, shamanism began to be persecuted by the Buddhists. Shamanism went underground, while Buddhism continued at work on the surface level of culture as a state religion. Buddhism manipulated the socio-politico-economic power of the state. However, shamanism continued to meet the masses' popular felt-needs. Gradually, it also developed cultural concepts of paradise, reincarnation, and palcha, as well as the concept of sacred and profane in the deeper structure of culture. As Buddhism secularized with socio-politico-economic power, both Buddhism and the state were corrupted.

The people's interest shifted from other worldly religion to this worldly religion. The founder of the Yi Dynasty realized the need for a conceptualized religion for the new state in order to replace a failed Buddhism. Thus, Confucianism became the new state religion attempting to meet the this-worldly and other-worldly needs of the Korean masses.

The Confucian Dimension

Confucianism was adopted during the Yi Dynasty, playing an important role in the dynasty's formation and taking Buddhism's place in becoming the nation's official ideology. From the beginning, Confucian officials endeavored to eradicate Buddhist elements from imperial politics.

Introduction of Confucianism

Confucianism was imported into Korea as early as the Three Kingdom period (ca. 57 B.C.– 668 A.D.) but was overshadowed by Buddhism and shamanism. In 682 A.D. a National Confucian School was established in the Silla Kingdom. King Kwangjong established the system of Confucianism examinations patterned after San Hsui (958 A.D.) of China. In 991 A.D. the first national shrine was erected in Sajik to venerate the Confucian sages. In 992 A.D. the King established Kugjakam, the college of the elites, and Munmyo the Confucian temple (Moon 1974: 19).

In 1392 A.D. Songgye Yi took over the throne of the Koryo kingdom, establishing the Yi Dynasty and adopting Confucianism as the state ideology and state religion. The elimination of the authority and influence of Buddhism and Buddhist temples was one of the primary tasks for the new dynasty. The royal court adopted the policy of expelling Buddhism and adopting Confucianism from 1401 to 1418 (Hei Chu Kim 1982:89). The Yi Dynasty used Neo-Confucianism as a means of maintaining political, social and economic order.[1]

Orthodoxy or Ideology

Confucianism is not so much a religion as it is a philosophy of life and an ethical and moral system. It is based on the five Chinese classical books of Confucianism: *Sijeon* (the Book of Odes), *Shooking* (the Scripture of Documents), *Juyeok* (the Book of Change), *Chunchu* (the Chronicles of Lu) and *Yeki* (the Book of Rites).

Confucian orthodoxy is very rational. Hei Chu Kim explains three basic views in Confucianism. First, the universe is characterized by order, regularity, and a harmonious integration of its parts. Second, it is possible for people to discern this order that underlies things and events. Third, one must be able to devote oneself to the systematic study of man, institutions, history, and the classics. This is the high calling of the "gentleman," the occupation that enables people to live in harmony with each other and the universe (1982:92).

Confucius postulated five virtues and five fundamental relationships. The five virtues are benevolent love, righteousness, proper conduct, wisdom, and faithfulness. Proper worship of heaven, nature, and ancestors was important to maintain harmony of the cosmic order. The five fundamental relationships are sovereign to subject, father to son, husband to wife, elder to younger, and friend to friend. To keep proper relationship between these pairs, Confucius laid down the five articles of morality and ethics: intimacy, differences, righteousness, obedience, and faithfulness. When people observe these principles, the world and its societies carry on harmoniously, peacefully and in order. In actual practice Confucian orthodoxy of the Yi Dynasty of Korea systematically fossilized the hierarchy of the state.

Orthopraxy of Neo-Confucianism: Effect on Social Structure

When the Yi Dynasty executed Neo-Confucianism in its socio-politico-economic structure, it affected the norms and values of social and familial systems. Consequently, it produced a ruler-subject mentality, an elite-oriented education system, a class-oriented society, as well as ancestral veneration.

The Ideology of Confucianism. Confucian orthodoxy diffused into the socio-economic-political structure of Korean society as a fundamental system. The royal government adopted the Neo-

71

Confucian theory of Chu Hsi from China and established this system as the norm for relations of people, state, and society to the cosmic order. Neo-Confucianism promoted ascriptive values, such as loyalty to one's ruler, filial piety to one's parents, and hierarchical relationships of subordination of wife to husband, younger friend to older friend, younger brother to elder brother (Chai-sik Chung 1982:100).

The principle of hierarchical relationships became the highest human and social value. The Yi Dynasty fossilized Neo-Confucianism as an ideological basis for social order, land reforms, and a centralized hierarchical state. This hierarchy fundamentally divided into emperor, chief ministers, high officials, gentlemen-scholars, and commoners. These hierarchical relationships necessitated a title-oriented society. The all-important title bestowed status to the individual. Even today Koreans call each other by the title of a present job or former position, such as "teacher," "president," "section chief," "department chief," "pastor," "elder," "deacon," or "director," followed by their family name.

Yangban and Sangmin Classes. In this social order the elite class, yangban (land owner scholar-official class) rose to high prominence on the social pyramid. Although orthodox Confucianism deeply saturated the lives of the Korean masses through moral and ethical teaching, educationally it remained a system for teaching the elite yangban, not the sangmin (commoners) (Chung 1982:101–102).

Sangmin were the uneducated low caste masses. They were commoners, peasants, or tenants. The feudalistic and imperialistic social structure produced by Confucianism left *sangmin* at the bottom. According to the concept of ruler-subject, absolute loyalty and subordination were required by the *sangmin* to the *yangban* classes. Theoretically, *sangmin* were allowed to take civil examinations to enter officialdom, but *chunmin* (the lowly born) were excluded from any form of political power (Man-Gap Lee 1982:34–37).

Kwageo System. *Kwageo* is a bureaucratic examination or civil examination to enter officialdom. Resting heavily on the bureaucratic structure of the Yi Dynasty, the *Kwageo* system was established to emphasize Confucian teaching on morals, ethics, and religion. Village elementary schools, local district schools, and the highest national college were also Confucian institutions. The *Kwageo* system promoted an elitist education system. If one could pass the *Kwageo* examination, their socio-politico-economic status would be totally changed to a higher position. Thus, concentrated study for the *Kwageo* examination was a life-long goal for many in the Yi Dynasty. This system was abolished in 1895, though the *Kwageo* mentality has continued into modern days in the form of an elitist school system. If one graduates from a prestigious school, he or she can get a prestigious job with high social status and marry into a wealthy family. That is why Korean parents still drive their children to earn straight A's and graduate from prestigious universities, even after they immigrate to America.

Family Structure: Filial Piety. The concept of ruler-subject, which formed the superstructure of the imperial system, also formed the substructure of the family system. The ruler-subject principle of relationships included father as ruler and son as subject; likewise, the husband ruled the wife. Absolute subordination was a cardinal virtue.

Ancestor veneration already existed, yet it was further codified and reinforced by Confucian principles and ceremonies. In order to reinforce and sustain ethical and moral principles, the Yi Dynasty promulgated written rites of induction, marriage, burial, and sacrifice.

The idea of filial piety is *hyo*, which includes children's reverence for their parents and caring for the parents in repayment for their parent's kindness in their upbringing. The concept was not an emotional or blood relation, but rather an ethical norm that extended from the king down to the common people of the whole society (Hui-Dok Yi 1973:10). It was a concept considered ontologically true even of the entire universe. Filial piety bound family and society together and governed all the rites. Filial piety surpassed even the loyalty concept in the sense that even emperors or kings were to display filial piety. The strong emphasis on filial piety accentuated the patriarchal, extended and traditional family systems. Self-sacrifice and loyalty were in turn preserved by the family and integrated into Korean nationalism. Social integration of families was achieved through organization of familial, social and religious rituals (Cf. Grant S. Lee 1976:21–23).

Yuji, An Informal Leader. *Yuji* is the non-official leadership that rules communal life and rites. It is the outcome of social integration of families. Every village, social unit, family, and ritual organization has a *yuji*, who is an opinion leader from the *yangban* or wealthy class. *Yuji* are located in and function in every Korean community. During the national election time (both presidential and parliamentary), campaigners seek the support of the *yuji*, assuming their underlying power will influence the general public's opinions. Every communal event is supported by *Yuji* as well as by the official leadership (Cf. Man Gap Lee 150).

Persecution of Folk Religion. Besides Buddhism there were different folk religions in Korea, particularly Taoism and shamanism. The Taoist cult was associated with divination, geomancy, and astrology. Taoists believed they could manipulate cosmic forces to attain good health, longevity, and good fortune. The Confucian Yi Dynasty disfavored and suppressed Buddhism, Taoism, and shamanism. Confucian scholar-officials were primarily preoccupied with this-worldly problems, particularly how they could induce filial obedience in the people through ancestral veneration. Other-worldly problems of salvation, religious experience, and magical or superstitious manipulation of spirits, were not their concern (Chung 1982:103).

My Own Case of Ancestral Veneration

I myself came from a background of ancestral veneration. I had been immersed in it all my life until l was converted to Christ. My grandfather was a Confucian priest, and he performed orthodox ancestral veneration on the various ancestral memorial days. These ancestral worship times were times of reunion for our family, relatives and clan. We listened and learned about our ancestors' good deeds. Such days were considered sacred and solemn for us.

In these rituals the invocation of spirits (*chesa* and *charye* rituals) climaxed the rituals of ancestral veneration, which were done at home. But *sihyang* rituals (annual collective clan rituals) were held in graveyards of remote villages of other regions, where our collective ancestral graveyards were located. My kinsmen or clans must have lived there. *Sihyang* was performed every fall in front of those ancestral graves. All ancestral veneration committee leaders would gather together and offer sacrifices. Later on they would discuss lineage, genealogy and business. Korean children look forward to these days of *chesa*, because they are treated better and eat better food than usual. The adults and children live for *chesa*, performing filial duties and expecting blessing from the venerated ancestors.

Summary of Confucian Dimension

Confucian rationalism is closely associated with this-worldliness. It involves prudent care for the interests of this world. It lacks interest in the afterlife and repudiates irrational or transcendent beliefs and practices. It also emphasizes the examination of moral and ethical problems over the scientific experimentation of the western world. Yet it retains a latent empiricism, which demands formulae to prove facts. Confucianism does not hold any doctrine of sin and salvation; therefore, there is no future security or present guidance. There is also no concept of repentance, forgiveness, adoption, or redemption.

In Confucianism, there is only right and wrong, honor and shame. There are no deities, gods, or spirits, only the supreme being (closely parallel to shamanism's Hananim). Related to people's felt needs, ancestral veneration was the only recognized means in Confucianism through which people could seek guidance, security, prosperity, or fertility. Because Confucianism has no theological distinctions, it maintains no obstacle to being wed with ancestral veneration and other aspects of shamanism. Any family who venerates ancestors will likely be involved in shamanism as well. The shaman becomes the medium of the ancestral spirits in necromantic practices (see above discussion of shamanism). Therefore, the orthopraxy of Neo-Confucianism invites veneration of ancestral spirits.

Confucianism began as a this-worldly ideology of ethical and moral formulae, a mechanistic analogy, but later it synthesized to other-worldly spirit worship, more of an organic analogy. People regarded dead ancestors as being alive as long as they were remembered. These dead ancestors were supposed to assist, reward, and punish their offspring according to their offspring's good or bad deeds (Hilbert 1987:65–67).

The Christian Dimension

Korean worldview shifted from the Buddhistic to Confucian dimensions along with government patronage without ever meeting the common people's felt needs. As a result of Confucianism, the nation was bound in a bureaucratic socio-politico-economic system. The common people, suffering from poverty and oppression, were open to receive blessing and freedom. Those who brought the gospel came from wealthy, free western nations.

The Beginning

I chose to review Protestantism rather than Catholicism, which was imported to Korea in 1784. The royal government rejected Catholicism and persecuted it. As a result of this persecution, Korea was for a century closed to any international western contact (Kwang Rin Lee 1976a:19–20). Therefore, my interest is in reviewing Christianity as brought by Protestant missionaries, which was well accepted and has been growing rapidly for about 100 years.

In 1875, two Scottish Presbyterian missionaries stationed in China, John Ross and John McIntyre, began to learn Korean from Lee-Eung Hyun. With Hyun's help, a Bible translation from Chinese to Korean was soon underway. By 1882, the Gospels of Luke and John were completed and smuggled to Korea. Bible translation was an ongoing enterprise. By 1887 the New Testament was completed (Chan Hie Kim 1982:118–119).

In 1885, Horace Underwood and Henry Appenzeller came to Korea as the first missionaries carrying the Gospel of Mark, which had been translated with the help of Soo Jung Lee by the American Bible Society in Yokohama. In 1889, the Korean Tract Society was organized by pioneering missionaries (Chan Hie Kim 1982:119). The evangelization of Korea was now firmly underway.

Persecution and Growth Under the Japanese

According to Orr's records, the Korean revival began in August 1903 at a missionary conference at Wonsan, a conference repeated in 1904 and in 1905. The second revival swept Korea in 1905–06. These awakenings had a significant effect upon church growth (Orr 1975:27).

In 1919, the Independence Movement against the colonialist Japanese was inspired by American President Woodrow Wilson's plea for self-determination. Since Christians were leading the movement, Imperialist Japanese police reacted with brutality and severe, systematic persecution of the church. A demonstration for freedom ended with indiscriminate, cruel bloodshed and mass imprisonment of hundreds of Christians, both leaders and participants. In one case they set fire to a church full of people. Many were also imprisoned (A. Clark 1971:199).

Out of this persecution, the Korean church experienced dramatic growth; both Methodists and Presbyterians more than doubled by 1920. In 1927, another revival broke out through the work of a young Methodist evangelist, Young-Do Lee, and began spreading all over Korea (Orr 1975:53). Through evangelistic campaigns, Bible reading, and witnessing, the church increased rapidly. Revival continued through 1928, but in 1930 the Japanese government forced Shinto worship on the churches and schools. Many who resisted Shinto worship were thrown into prison and suffered severe and cruel torture. Yet the church kept growing anyway. Blair recorded that "more than two hundred Christian leaders died a martyr's death during the War" (1957:106). Duk-Whang Kim wrote that 2000 church leaders were imprisoned during the Second World War (1988:397). Later Orr reflected on that persecution positively, "In Korea, a persecuted church provided the spiritual backbone for a nation" (1975:53).

In 1945 Korea regained her freedom from the shackles of imperial colonization, yet the political tragedy was not solved entirely—Korea was now divided between North and South. In 1945, revival led by a leading evangelist, Sung Bong Lee, resulted in church growth, but the Communists were already beginning to arrest Christian leaders in the north.

Communist Persecution

The influx of North Korean refugees infused South Korean Christians with a spirit of prayer, which helped prepare them for war. In 1950 the Korean War broke out. By the time the cease-fire was signed in 1953, the country was devastated. However, by 1958 the Church was again showing amazing growth. By 1960 thirty million copies of the Bible had been published and distributed, one copy for every person in South Korea. In 1973 the Billy Graham crusade drew crowds of over one million in attendance.

The Church at Present

In 1985, the Korean Church celebrated her centennial. Currently the world' s largest Presbyterian, Pentecostal, Methodist, and Baptist churches are in Seoul. The Korean Church still aims to evangelize ten million through a program called the "million evangelization movement." 1985 statistics show the whole Christian population at 9,736,396. Protestants compromised 34.24 percent of the religious population and 13.24 percent of the total population according to the statistics of the Department of Korean Communication and Literature in 1984. Protestant denominations multiplied to sixty-nine and the Protestant clergy stood at 40,717 (Department of Korean Communication and Literature, Jan., 1984).

Korean Christianity: Other-Worldly and This-Worldly

Traditionally, Korea had no education system for the common people except for the village classes. While traditional education was developed for the elite, general education was rejected, a direct result of Confucianism and Neo-Confucianism. Western style education was begun by the first Christian missionaries, who laid the foundation of modern Korean education. Mary Scranton started a girl's school, Ewha Hakdang, and a boy's school, BaeJae Hakdang, to propagate the Christian faith and to train leadership. In fact most missionaries started schools as soon as they began their missionary work. By 1909 the Presbyterians had 14,708 students in 605 institutions, while the Methodists had 200 schools with 6432 students, and other denominations opened 950 schools (Kyung Bae Min 1972:35–43).

The dramatic figures show the significant contribution Christian education has made to the modernization of Korea. Indeed, after Korea became a Japanese colony, two other types of schools appeared: public and private. Mission schools aimed to train Christian leaders or to convert people to Christ, while Japanese public schools aimed to produce skillful, functional, and obedient colonized people. In spite of the Japanese schools, the majority of Korean students wanted liberation, and united their hearts in pursuit of independence (Min 1981:198).

The spirit of the missionary education is captured by these words of missionary James E. Fisher, who served in Korea from 1919 to 1935:

> The Western culture is not to supersede or displace the Korean culture, but to supplement and modify it, whenever and whatever it is found desirable in terms of greater values to do so. It is assumed that in all of his cooperation with the Koreans, the missionary is learning as well as teaching.... Since the missionary is the emissary from a foreign land, however, since he is in the position of a teacher, it is natural to suppose that he has something of special value for the Koreans, and something which he can bring them which they might not otherwise get (1970:53–54).

With this philosophy, he suggested that the best features of Western education be emphasized in Korea: the organization of thought and scientific knowledge, leading to the introduction of technical, industrial, artistic, and literary pursuits as well as political, religious, and social knowledge. Griffis also made a notable observation:

> The education which the American pioneers, led by Appenzeller, incarnated...began instantly to supply a crying need and to minister to the mental, social and political diseases of the nation. It taught the pupil to think. It transferred the emphasis of training from the memory to the judgment. It transformed sight into insight. It taught pupils to inquire into cases and master in practice the eternal law of cause and effect. It put a premium on manliness and chivalry...and set value, in both rewards and honours, upon honest toil, even with the hands (1912:178).

Korean mission schools which emphasized religion, sociology, education, politics, and ethical education made a tremendous impact on the modernization of the nation. Kwang Rin Lee quotes Jae-pil Suh's editorial in the *Tongnip Newspaper*: "Countries whose peoples believe in Christianity are [sic] strongest, wealthiest, most civilized and most enlightened in the world; and they live under great blessings of God" (1976b:32). From his point of view, Christianity made Western nations the wealthiest and strongest. Lee describes progressive thinker Pak Younhyo's attitudes towards Christianity: "He was firmly convinced that Christianity was a necessary religion for the education of the Korean people" (1976b:32).

Acceptance of the Gospel

When Christianity was introduced, it was already evident that Buddhism had ruined the state and was not able to meet the felt needs of people, while Confucianism brought up and nurtured a culture of bureaucracy and hierarchy from family life to the royal court. Confucianism, furthermore, had created a severe caste society, segregating and fossilizing the categories of the system under the presumed cosmic order of Confucianistic principles (Chung 1982:106). By the end of the Yi Dynasty, the masses resented and rebelled against the *yangban* system; they were hungry to have a new religion which might release them from the Confucian feudal system (Kwang Rin Lee 1976b:38).

The early Protestant missionaries offered a new, concrete and certain theology of creation, redemption, salvation, heaven and hell, and eternal life through Christ Jesus. For the first time, Koreans heard of and accepted the personal Almighty God. Man Gap Lee says of these missionaries, "They established schools and hospitals as well as churches and actively proselytized. In this way they provided many cultural benefits" (1982:59).

To Koreans, the Christian gospel liberated them from sin, the bondage and fear of spirits; and the social caste system. The gospel of Christ was good news to nearly every segment of the society. It was fiercely rejected by some Confucian scholars, but they were already losing their influence on people. Through Christianity, new waves of Western civilization and modernization were surging beyond all resistance. Koreans, "people of the old hermit nation," were wide open to the changes of a new religion and new era.

The Power of Christianity

For Koreans the power of the gospel was that of reconciliation from enmity between God and themselves, and redemption from hell to heaven by grace, in contrast to the Buddhist works-oriented *nirvana*. The power of the Holy Spirit was the power of victory over the spirits, and the masses were liberated from a preoccupation with *palcha*. Christianity also meant liberation from the social caste system, as well as giving hope for liberation from foreign powers. Christianity offered not only the security of eternal life, but the Kingdom of God also brought inner peace, joy, and love into the hearts of those who received it. Of course, the first converts were targets of persecution because of their rejection of ancestral veneration.

Christianity and Great Cultural Changes

As a result of Christianity's impact on Korea, the people began to foster democratic ideals and rational thinking, both privately and openly. Korea began to see its traditional beliefs and customs as being unscientific and unproductive ideas that blocked the way to material gain and westernization (Cf. Man Gap Lee 1982:59–60). Christianity brought changes in traditional inequalities between the sexes, which under Confucianism had put women in an almost slave-like position. Christianity brought a greater sense of equality through the grace of God and broke down the idea of a wall between men and women, the privileged and the under privileged.

Korean women previously had no socially accepted identities of their own but were known as a man's daughter, mother or wife. The Christian gospel brought women out of the home, taught them the Bible, and gave them an education in mission schools. Girls' mission schools accelerated Social changes toward equality, and women began participating in society. Accordingly, concubines and polygamy were gradually abolished by imperatives of Christianity and modern education. Due to elevation of women's status, the roles of women increased and diversified, expanding their job opportunities and involvement in social activities (Man Gap Lee 1982:107–108).

Christianity brought reformation to the social structure. According to Man Gap Lee there were seven social casts: royalty, *yangban* (nobility), *hyangban* (gentry), *chungin* (middle folk), *so-ol* (illegitimate sons of the nobility), *sangmin* (low cast), and *chunmin* (outcast). Christianity broke these barriers (1982:34). Missionaries were not blind to these social realities, but they chose to disregard the social classes of the people they contacted. Different classes sang and worshipped together and received education together.

In 1910 Korea was forcibly annexed to Japan and became a colony. Korean Christians fell under great suffering and persecution from the Japanese rulers. Korean Christian leaders made a great impact in the Independence Movement against Japanese colonial government in 1919, and this powerfully motivated Koreans to be open to the gospel. Out of the crushing of the Independence Movement, the church grew even more rapidly through the patriotic example and prominent role of Christians in the movement, as well as many powerful Christian witnesses of spiritual blessings during imprisonment. This movement brought very "favorable publicity to the Christian cause" (Alfred Wasson 1934:101). The endless suffering from oppression and war brought increased openness to the gospel.

As Christianity grew, barriers of social classes continued to diminish. And out of modernization and socio-cultural changes traditional belief systems and structures changed. Also nationalism, pragmatism, individualism, materialism and anti-communism rose up in the process of westernization.

Indigenization of Korean Christianity

Right after national liberation, the Korean church experienced the pain of communist persecution and of a nation severed between north and south. In this context Charismatic and holiness movements exploded greatly (Min 1981:471). Many Charismatic ministers emerged, followed by fervent mass evangelism. Some of these Korean church movements emphasized indigenization and bordered on syncretism with shamanism (Min 1981:399). These sects included Tae Sun Park's Olive Tree sect, Sun Myung Moon's

Unification Church, and others calling for "mysticism and spiritism." They began to appear and mislead the masses into divergent heresies (Min 1981:471).

Many prayer mountains were established, where Christians read the Bible, fasted, and prayed to receive the power of the Holy Spirit. The Korean Church began to grow, the worldview of believers gained a more biblical orientation, and the healing of incurable diseases and demonstration of signs and wonders was frequent.

Syncretism with shamanistic beliefs has always been a dangerous pitfall for Korean Christianity, and more so are other-worldly Buddhist concepts and cravings for this-worldly blessings. The Christian church simply cannot say, "that's shamanism" and despise it, because people perpetually seek power, security and guidance.

Koreans have become "modernized," leading to materialism, individualism, and pragmatism. Modernization commenced concurrently with the coming of Christianity. The changes in the social structure, symbolized by high-rise buildings dominating the large cities, are due to radical urbanization, which accelerated change almost beyond imagination.

The spread of the gospel was expedited by the deep sense of filial piety. If a new convert was the family head, the whole family often followed his decision. If a child was converted, because of the filial piety concept, the child prayed and fasted for their parents' salvation. The parents would do the same for their unsaved children. The discipline of prayer life in Buddhism and spiritism enabled Koreans to become saturated in a prayer life centering on Christ, as well as having a built-in awareness of the spirit world. Within a century, one-third of the whole nation became Christian. How Christianity met this-worldly and other-worldly needs of people should be analyzed.

Christianity Meets This-Worldly and Other-Worldly Needs

Christianity was brought to Korea by Westerners who rarely understood the this-worldly supernatural dimension of what Hiebert calls the "middle zone" (See Hiebert 1982:39–46).[2] Even though Korean Christians understood the reality of demons prior to conversion, once they became Christian, they were taught to ignore the middle zone.

Since Buddhism appealed to the upper class and was taught in monasteries as an other-worldly religion, it was not a religion that the masses could apply to their daily lives. Instead, they went to Buddhistic or shamanistic shrines, towers and images and, rubbing their hands, they prostrated themselves before useless images in search of solutions to their problems.

Confucianism, as an elitist and purely this-worldly ideology, shifted the focus from Buddhism's other-worldly focus. Confucianism offered a new belief and practice intended to create equilibrium and cosmic harmony. But due to the ideological and rational nature of Confucianism, it was incapable of explaining other-worldly problems of death, life, sickness, and calamity. Buddhist and Confucian worldviews simply blended with and added to the deep-level shamanism of daily life.

The Holy Spirit and Pentecostal movements, and the prayer mountain emphasis brought a re-awareness of demonic realities. Through the gifts of the Holy Spirit, ministry expanded to meet the wider felt needs of the people for physical and inner healing. Christianity has proved capable of meeting both other-worldly and this-worldly needs.

There is no way to understand what makes people respond so positively to the gospel without taking into account the humanistic, Buddhistic, and Confucian streams so fundamental to Korean worldview. To evangelize Koreans in their own Korean context requires knowledge of these factors I have discussed.

Beyond this, to reach new immigrants with the gospel a further dimension must be understood. That is the tension brought about by being new to the American worldview and lifestyle while still being driven by all that is fundamentally Korean. In the following chapter we shall review ways in which Korean and American worldview themes conflict. This will inevitably affect the problems, which we have encountered in the Nazarene Churches in Southern California.

Chapter 6

COMPARISON OF KOREAN AND AMERICAN WORLDVIEW THEMES

The deep level realities of the Korean world are not left behind when immigrating from Korea to America. We shall look at five major areas of difference between Korean and American worldviews, which will help to explain their differences: Self and other, relationship, classification, causality, and space and time (Kearney 1984:68–107).

Since worldview is the mental window to look at the world, it causes the "why" question toward other people's behavior. Several American pastors have asked me, "Why do Koreans have to eat meals together after services and make the room smell of *kimchi*?" "Why are Korean children undisciplined and always running around the church?" "Why do the Koreans like to worship only in the sanctuary and always pray at the church?" These are legitimate questions for Americans but needless for Koreans, because they are obviously natural behavior for Koreans. These questions arise due to different assumptions of time, space, and relationships, which are important worldview themes.

Since Koreans have been thoroughly enculturated with the different ideas of what is sacred and what is profane, it is easy for them to apply these principles to their understanding of biblical holiness. Therefore, Koreans prefer to pray in front of an altar rather than in an ordinary room, and they prefer to worship in a sanctuary rather than in a common meeting hall.

Space and Time

Concepts of space and of time are fundamentally different between Korean and American worldviews. One makes clear distinctions; the other does not.

Korea: Sacred and Profane

The concept of sacred and profane is applied to both time and place. The Korean word used to express the concept of profane is *bujeong hadda*. When domestic animals (oxen, pigs, dogs, cats, rabbits) reproduce, it is a sacred time, and the animal's owners pay special attention that the animal does not become "unclean." Traditional Korean farmers believe that if a menstruating woman goes to the location where an ox or pig is giving birth, the event becomes unclean. As a result, the spirit of fertility will be angered and demand that they kill and eat the newborn animal, because the woman is considered unclean and has violated sacred time and place. Women must be equally cared for when giving birth. When a baby is born, people who have attended a funeral are not to visit the newborn or the family for seven or fourteen days. This is because the unclean spirit could attach itself to the baby or mother.

Space. The term "space" can be understood geographically or it can be perceived metaphorically, that is, psychologically or mathematically (Kearney 1984:92). Different worldviews have very different concepts of space. According to Eliade, "For religious man, space is not homogeneous; he experiences interruptions, breaks in it; some parts of space are qualitatively different from others" (1959:20).

The religious person "brackets" space in his religious experience. This space becomes sacred, significant, and non-homogeneous-a special world in which the religious person encounters the ontological sacred manifestation of absolute reality.

This phenomenon occurs throughout the Bible. When God appears to Moses and to Joshua, He tells them to take off their shoes because they are on holy ground (Ex.3:5; Josh.5:15). The Bible frequently uses the terms "consecration," "holy," and "clean" when speaking of places, people, garments, objects, or instruments in the temple.

Eliade contrasts this with the profane experience, in which "space is homogeneous and neutral; no break qualitatively differentiates the various parts of its mass" (1959:22). For non-religious people a place is not significant or different from any other in a spiritual sense. Only in an historical or memorable or respective sense is it qualitatively different.

The Korean primitive religion of animism mixed with shamanism profoundly stimulated the development of the concept of sacred and profane from the beginning of the ancient tribal nation. According to ancient historical documents in Korea (*Samkuk Saki* and *Samkuk Yusa*), ancient tribal people held prayer rites to heavenly spirits with food and dancing through the 10th month of the lunar year (Moon 1982:18). The rules developed for these rites concerned the time, place and objects of the rites. People conceptualized space through a thorough integration of religion into their lives.

In shamanistic rituals, purification rites are performed at the beginning of the event to purify the place and people so they may have union with the spirits. Similar concepts of the profane are also found in Buddhism and Confucianism. Wives prepare themselves with bathing and a vegetarian diet for three days poor to Buddhist rites for familial blessings of longevity, good luck and prosperity.

When preparing food for Confucian ancestral rites, wives are extremely careful not to let any hairs or fragments of stone enter the sacrificial food, for anything profane or unclean is believed to provoke the anger of ancestral spirits who would bring disaster upon the family. The term *bujeong tada* is used frequently in daily conversation: "Don't touch it, *bujeong ta!*" ("you'll make it unclean") expresses the deep interrelationship between the clean and the unclean, or profane. The concept of profane lies deep within the subconscious of the Korean mind.

Korean men do not sit at the corner of a table, because the corner is considered taboo for men. Korean men are supposed to sit at the center of the table. A man's body also has certain parts that are thought to be more sacred than others. A man's shoulders, neck and head are considered sacred. It is taboo for children or women to touch his head or shoulders. Touching these parts will bring bad luck. If a woman or girl steps on a man's shoes, the man would expect bad luck to follow, because a man's feet are more sacred than those of a woman.

Shamanism relates closely to women and traditional Korean homes. It is primarily a women's religion; men are only superficially involved. Thus, traditional Korean homes have come to serve as shamanistic sanctuaries. In this respect traditional Korean homes and their grounds are regarded as sacred places. In traditional Korean homes the spaces considered most sacred are the shrine, altar and *jang dokdae* (storage platform for traditional Korean hot pepper and soy sauce).

Thus, the design of a traditional Korean house is different from that of an American home. There is no master bedroom in a traditional Korean house; instead there is one for the family head with an inner chamber for the housewife. The inner chamber or courtroom, the most sacred place in the house, is the place where traditional rituals are done, since in traditional Korean thinking the home is a sacred place due to the pantheon of house gods. The sacred nature of houses is one reason they do not wear shoes in the house.

Public space is also perceived differently. City plans and administrational system divisions are different. Therefore, street signs are marked and used differently from the American way. In public places certain spaces are set apart if they relate to shamanism, Buddhism, or Confucianism.

In traditional Korean culture people also believe in sacred places in nature. Cedar, gingko, and pear trees were considered sacred due to folk tales. Spirits were believed to dwell in the mountains, mountain paths, water, houses, earth, and wind. Thus, particular mountains, paths, wells, and places in houses were considered sacred and became locations for shrines where shamanistic rituals were held. These concepts were syncretized with Buddhism and Confucianism to further develop the principles of the sacred and profane by bracketing times and places as being set apart for encounters with gods.

Even Christians today often consider wedding ceremonies sacred in the above-mentioned ways. Someone who has attended funeral rites might not subsequently participate in a wedding because of the profanity of death. I know one believer, a Mrs. Kim, who did not attend her church members' funeral, because she was planning to attend her daughters' wedding. Thus, she avoided that profane rite which could bring bad luck for her daughter's wedding. She is a deaconess of a church and a committed believer, yet her worldview of the sacred and profane remains largely unchanged.

The Korean mind developed sacred spatial concepts similar to biblical concepts of holiness and the notion of being "set apart." Thus, the church sanctuary is very significant, and retreats to *kidowon* (prayer mountains) for prayer and fasting are very popular. Koreans strive to secure and maintain a holy place and time for their communion with the Holy God.

Time. Time is bracketed according to worldviews of sacred and profane such bracketing is practiced everyday. Yet it is practiced in everyday life. Eliade elaborates on the profane duration and sacred time in the religious person's heart:

> For religious man time too, like space, is neither homogeneous nor continuous. On the one hand there are the intervals of a sacred time, the time of festivals (by far the greater part of which are periodical); on the other there is profane time, ordinary temporal duration, in which acts without religious meaning have their setting. Between these two kinds of time there is, of course, solution of continuity; but by means of rites, religious man can pass without danger from ordinary temporal duration to sacred time (1959:68).

Religious festivals or rituals are the reenactment of a sacred event that took place in a mythical past time. Time is bracketed into sacred periods of union with gods. Similarly, Christian rituals are times of communion with God in worship, retreat, or Holy Communion. The day on which ancestral worship is held is considered sacred, because ancestral spirits are visiting their offspring in order to receive worship. Therefore, the women who prepare the food that day should be very solemn and clean.

New Year's Day is considered sacred, along with the whole week following it. Except for a New Year courtesy call, people are not supposed to visits. In rural farm houses three spadesful of red dirt are kept in front of the door on particular sacred days of January (lunar calendar) in order to ward people away.

Kearney divides images of time into oscillating time and linear time (1984:98–99). Oscillating time is also called cyclical time, which stresses the repetition of events (Hiebert 1987:40). The word "cyclical" implies revolving or circular movement, which begets a great deal of repetition in birth, life, death, and rebirth. E.R. Leach depicts oscillating time:

> There is no sense of going on and on in the same direction, or round and round the same wheel. On the contrary, time is experienced as something discontinuous, a repetition of repeated reversal, a sequence of oscillations between polar opposites: night and day, winter and summer, drought and flood, age and youth, life and death. In such a scheme the past has no depth to it, all past is equally past; it is simply the opposite of now (1966:126).

Koreans think in cyclical time, which encompasses life, death and rebirth, in a word, transmigration. The Korean concept of time (*yukkap*)[1] came from *The Book of Change*, Chinese *Yin/Yang* theory and the five elements, which are divided time into two hour periods on the modern clock. Each hour was symbolized by an animal: rat, cow, tiger, dragon, snake, goat, horse, sheep, monkey, rooster, dog, and rabbit. Each animal symbolized distinct fortunes, characters and traits. These same animals were represented by calendrical dates, months, and years. Therefore, as much as possible, it was a must for traditional parents for a child to be born at a good hour, date month, and year. A Korean father would wait a year to register a baby girl if she had been born in a tiger or horse year, because this would supposedly bring bad fate to the family as well as herself.

Korean time is repetitiously cyclical as well as being "polychronic." According to Edward Hall, in polychronic time several things happen at once, and stress is on involving people and completing transactions rather than adhering to preset schedules. He adds that "polychronic time is apt to be considered a point rather than a ribbon or a road, and that present point is sacred" (1981a:17).

The most sacred time of day for Koreans is the break of dawn. If a person has an eye illness, he or she is supposed to look eastward at the dawn and bow toward the sun three times so that he or she may be healed. If a person whispers a wish after bowing three times toward the rising sun on the first full moon day of the year, that person's wish is supposed to come true. Since morning is a sacred time, ancestral worship on the Korean thanksgiving day (Aug. 15th) and on New Year's Day are held in the morning. Also birthdays are celebrated with a big breakfast not with lunch or supper. Thus, Koreans are naturally enthusiastic about attending dawn prayer meetings, not only because of the biblical example, but also because it is natural within their cultural context.

Midnight to 2 a.m. (*Ja* [horse] hour) was also considered sacred, and ancestral worship was held at that hour. Presently, most adult Koreans come from this background of considering the midnight hour to be sacred. Thus, in addition to the biblical example, it is natural for every Korean church to hold a midnight prayer meeting.

During the Yi Dynasty the royal government rang bells every two hours (related the above mentioned system of *yukkap*). Thus, Korean notions of time, self and other, and relationship are deeply intertwined. Since each time space covered a two-hour span, the Koreans' sense of time is more relaxed and spatial than punctual. This accounts for "Korean time," which allows one to be 30 minutes to one hour without apology. Weddings or any kind of ceremony will always start from 30 minutes to an hour late, yet no one gets upset. This is one reason most Koreans struggle to keep up with the time-oriented American culture.

America: Secular Non-Distinction

While American Christians of traditional, particularly high church, denominations often feel a sense of sacredness in both space and time when they worship in a church sanctuary, Americans as a whole (primarily those of European descent) inherited little fundamental cultural distinction between sacred and profane from their ancestors. Thus, the average American, Christian or not, tends to treat times and places as being very much equal, not assigning any inherent distinction of sacredness or uncleanness.

91

Space. Americans tend to make few, if any, spatial distinctions between sacred and profane, preferring to see space as something to be utilized. What sacredness of space there is, is usually dependent on time (e.g., ceremonies and memories).

American spatial concepts are characterized by a general sense of equality. One place or location of an event may be more attractive than another, but it holds no greater or lesser degree of sacredness. Cleanness and uncleanness, whether at births, weddings, funerals, on parts of the body, or in buildings and geographical locations, is primarily identified not by the presence of spirits by the presence of dirt and germs.

Among Christians, church buildings hold some sacredness, but every other place is equal. In liturgical churches such as Roman Catholic, Episcopalian, Lutheran, and to a lesser degree Methodist and Presbyterian, there is a graduated sense of sacred space within the church. The most sacred places are the altar and platform for the clergy. The rest of the sanctuary where worshipers sit is less sacred, the vestibule is semi-sacred, and the sidewalk and street are secular (Cf. Hiebert 1987:99).

American people will sit on dining tables and desks as well as walk around the inside of a house with their shoes on, all of which is taboo in Korean culture. There is little sense of sacred boundaries around physical places. In some churches Americans even worship with shorts and bare feet. In Korean culture only a person who cannot afford to purchase a pair of shoes will walk around barefoot on the (unclean) street, while in warm weather some Americans will walk barefoot almost anywhere.

Neither mountain nor ocean is religiously sacred for an American. These are beautiful elements of nature, and are to be respected and cared for, but Americans do not perceive them to be sacred dwelling places of the gods as Koreans traditionally have. Function and beauty are much stronger foundations for the design and use of space than are any concepts of sacredness.

Time. Hiebert comments on how much more important time is to North Americans than space:

> The priority that North Americans place on time as against space is seen in our emphasis on history. We put dates on our checks and applications. We keep track of birthdays,

anniversaries, and other important events in our lives. It is hard, therefore, for us to understand people who see land and space as more important than time (1985:133).

American worldview understands time as being linear. Linear time is a uniform interval of time, having a beginning and an end. Hall describes the perception of time in the northern European tradition as being "linear and segmented like a road or a ribbon extending forward into the future and backward to the past" (1981a:19). Linear time has three distinct segments: past, present, and future. Since linear time is in a constant forward motion from one segment to another, it is irreversible and future oriented. American time has a clear past, present, and future tense; it travels only one way and is irreversible. By the same reasoning, the past cannot be regained and the present is but a transitory point traveling toward the future (Kearney 1984:101).

Therefore, once time is lost it cannot be regained, and the present moment should be given attention and value. Appointments are important as Hall clearly pointed out: "Once set, the schedule is almost sacred, so that it is wrong, according to the formal dictates of our culture, to be late, but it is a violation of the informal patterns to keep changing schedules or appointments or to deviate from agenda" (1981b:157).

American time is what he labeled "monochronic," i.e. doing one thing at a time. Monochronic time is characterized by emphasizing scheduling, segmentation, and promptness. By scheduling we compartmentalize and make it possible to concentrate on one thing at a time. But monochronic time can alienate us from our very selves and deny us the experience of our wider context.

Ever since Benjamin Franklin said that "time is money," people in industrial societies have carefully dealt with minutes and seconds (Kearney 1984:104). In everyday language, time is bought, lost, "spent," "earned," "made up," "saved," and "wasted." This American concept is rooted in Puritanism, and later "democratic faith works ethics." Gabriel comments: "It was preached in the eighteenth century.... Its advice to the young man was: work and save, if you would win the game of life and honor the God who made you. 'Work, for the Night is Coming' became a popular hymn of evangelical Protestantism" (1956:156).

Since time is money, if one does not organize his time, he wastes it and is not productive, thus losing money. If one does not produce, he is not a worthy member of society. In order to produce, one must spend time working, and by working, individuals acquire property and accumulate wealth. Wealth comes to those who have superior energy and ability to produce. Competition is unavoidable. Time orientation thus fuels competitive individualism in human relationships and influencing human behavior toward a mechanistic kind of materialism.

The image of linear time is mechanically regulated by the clock in industrial societies. Punctuality and discipline of time is a prime virtue for management. Clock-oriented American culture binds people in a harness of time and pushes them to be frequently under time pressure. De Grazia describes the American time concept:

> The American office schedule is tight and sacred too. "I will see you at four ten, then," is a sentence that would have been comprehensible to no other civilization this earth has seen. Violators of the schedule are punished. If you are not on time for appointments, you will come to be regarded as an irresponsible person. If a man is kept waiting in the outer office for ten or fifteen minutes, careful apologies are necessary (quoted in Kearney 1984:104).

Lewis Mumford discovered that this strong time scheduling and timeliness orientation coincided with the mass production of watches in Switzerland and later America during the mid 1800s. Furthermore, punctuality and accurate scheduling were requisite to produce, transport and sell products (1963:17).

In Korean culture people do not use the phrase, "wait a second." Rather, they say, "wait for a while." They have little concept of minutes or seconds; rather their concept is of a long or short while. American schedules tend to be punctual, but Koreans tend to be flexible. Koreans are more people oriented than time oriented (except in areas of industry, transport, and marketing where they are similar).

In the American mind sacred and profane concepts of time are absent, except for Sunday or other various festivals or holidays. Sunday is a holy day for Christians, yet after church American Christians might go to the beach or mountains or shop, while Korean Christians will restrain themselves from that. Many Koreans would feel they had profaned Sunday by going to the beach.

Causality

Concepts of causality are a second area of fundamental difference between Korean and American worldviews. One is essentially fatalistic; the other, scientific.

Korea: Palcha

The notion of causality in Korea is grounded in *palcha*,[2] which is the fundamental idea of fate in one's life. *Palcha* is the explanation of the power of cause and effect on a person's success or failure, fortune or disaster. Emile Durkheim defined causality this way: "The first thing which is implied in the notion of the causal relationship is the idea of efficacy, or productive power, of active force. By cause we ordinarily mean something capable of producing a certain change. The cause is the force before it has shown the power which is in it; the effect is the same power, only actualized" (Durkheim 1965:406).

A Korean "will be a Confucianist when in society, a Buddhist when he philosophizes, and a spirit worshiper when in trouble" (Hulbert 404–405). We must add that he will be a blamer of *palcha* in times of bad luck and misfortune. Therefore, one cannot ignore the concept of *palcha* in the study of Korean worldview. It is a belief of cosmic and mechanical forces that control human life, similar to *kismet* in Islamic contexts and *karma* in Hindu contexts.

In many conversations people will employ *palcha* to explain good and bad parents, spouses, prosperity and failures. This cosmic ideology of determining one's fate originates from "reading" the hour, day, month, and the year in which one was born, which I described in the previous section.

In Korea the principles of belief in cosmic forces derive from the "Great Ultimates" (Taeguk), which produced the well-known

95

philosophy of *yin/yang*, the fundamental, ontological and relational principles of change (Jung Young Lee 10).

Palcha, the system for explaining good and evil, comes from the *Book of Change* and views life as having a predetermined course. The Buddhistic idea of *karma*, which flourished for about 1500 years, confirmed the concept with a concrete explanation of reincarnation.

The importance of *palcha* is revealed in many different aspects of people's lives. In the year of the tiger or the year of the white horse, housewives endeavor not to be pregnant. A girl born in such a year will have difficulty finding a husband, because her *palcha* will be questionable. Thus, some parents will alter the date of birth by registering such a girl's birth the following year in order to hide the real year of birth with its problematic *palcha* (Alexandre Guillemoz 1973:17).

Palcha belief system leads to occultism, divination, and shamanism. On account of *palcha*, before marriage a couple takes the data of their births to a diviner, fortune teller, *mudang, pansu*, or *yubok* for the purpose of examining the unity or harmony of the couples' *saju*,[3] another aspect of *palcha*. *Saju* means the four pillars of causality in one's life: hour, day, month and year of birth. Thus, *palcha* is the most basic and fundamental concept in fortune telling. The *palcha* concept is so deeply ingrained in peoples' minds that people use the term daily to express their frustration of a bad situation. Even a Christian might slip and say, "My *palcha* is bad," as a passing comment.

Palcha has many facets of application, among which are the following:

1. Quality—the saying, "She has good *palcha*; therefore, she has a good husband," describes the quality of *palcha*. Frequently *palcha* is described as good, wild, rich, or bad.

2. Unavoidability—the saying, "One's fate is not deceivable," expresses that one cannot avoid *palcha*. This kind of language is so very frequent that, as we said, even Christians use it without giving it any thought, because *palcha* is a habitual way of explaining unavoidable occurrences.

3. Particularity—the saying, "Each one lives according to fate," expresses that each person's fate is uniquely different from others'.

4. Causality of reincarnation—the saying, "One does not know the sins of the former life which cause bad fate in this life," expresses the fatalism deeply related to Buddhistic ideologies of karma and reincarnation.

5. Conditionality—the saying, "A woman had her husband keep a concubine in order to avoid her misfortune decreed by fate," implies that having a bad sickness or traffic accident is supposed to deter a worse disaster later.

6. Alterability—the saying, "A widow altered her *palcha*," means that a widow married a new husband. This idea originated in contrast to the Confucian idea that she ought to remain as a widow for the rest of her life. "He made money and changed his *palcha*" depicts how a person got rich and rose to a better condition of life. One cannot be free from *palcha*, but one can change it through political power, money, marriage, or divination.

7. Social relationship—the saying, "Losing parents in early childhood is of fate," explains why a child is orphaned. When a girl is born in the year of the white horse and later loses her parents and later her husband, she is the victim of strong fate.

Since *palcha* is believed to be an impersonal, amoral force that causes success or failure in human life, people are free form social, personal and intentional culpability. They need only to blame palcha, under which they are in lifetime bondage.

America: Scientific Cause and Effect

Emil Durkheim describes causality in terms of an "effective power" that arises from the need of a society for its members to believe in the efficacy of its communal rites and practices through which the society is held together (quoted in Kearney 1984:85). While this may be more plainly exemplified in Korean religious rituals, in American culture Durkheim's hypothesis takes the form of a broad shift toward belief in science over religion in terms of everyday life.

In 1859 Charles Darwin published *The Origin of the Species*. Darwin, like Isaac Newton before him, made a significant social impact through scientific findings and theories. Darwin's hypothesis of the evolution of man, along with a contemporary rise in rationalism, cast doubts on the reliability of the Bible (Latourette 1975:1070). Darwinism paved the way for science to challenge Christianity and for secular humanism to use science as its foundation.

"The religion of humanity was, in a sense, the reappearance of the humanism and the faith in science and in reason of the eighteenth century Enlightenment" (Gabriel 1956:194). The religion of humanity was deeply reinforced and supported by John Dewey's pragmatic instrumentalism, in which he stressed the scientific method to discover truth. "Dewey's pragmatism was a method of eliminating concepts of a supernatural deity" (Gabriel 1956:348). In spite of receiving criticism, Dewey's pragmatism became pervasive and influential in the first half of the 20th century.

As Americans accepted scientism, "the revolt against old absolutism gathered momentum" (Gabriel 1956:411). Truth became no longer absolute and eternal; truth was in the changing and empirical course of events. Thus, American minds were becoming scientifically oriented, searching for rational and empirical causes and effects. The theological implications of a rational and empirical worldview led to scientific reductionism in interpreting Scripture, which, in return, led to anti-supernaturalism in liberal Christianity, and to a lesser degree in many conservative Christian circles.

While many American Christians are quite aware of paranormal or supernatural causes and effects, others may be little different form non-Christians in terms of their view of scientific cause and effect. For example, they may depend upon doctors in time of illness without requesting God to heal. They may also go to counselors or psychologists for emotional or psychological problems rather than seek God's help or consider possibilities of problems in the spiritual realm.

Self and Other

Concepts of self and other are a third area of fundamental difference between Korean and American worldviews. One is essentially corporate, the other, individual.

Korea: Group Orientation

The origins of Korea's group orientation may be seen in its history. It is monoracial, monolinguistic, and monocultural, all of which lend themselves to social cohesiveness. Because the nation suffered repeated foreign invasions, particularly from China and Japan, countrymen had to be cohesive in solidarity to survive and to defend the nation. Through repeated national crises Koreans seem to have reinforced their corporate identity, extending from the family unit to the nation.

family →   village →   school →   company →   national →
self   self   self   self   self

In Korean culture the concept of self is understood only as being part of a family or group. Identity comes from the family, clan, village, school or company, even national selfhood. Children depend on parents and obey, and when the parents get old, they depend on the children, living with them in an extended family system. Therefore, marriage in traditional families is still a family affair that establishes a relationship between families, rather than a union of individuals. But divorce is now occurring in contemporary Korea. Yet if one member of the family goes through a divorce, it badly affects the family members who chose the spouse. Divorce is a failure and shame to the collective family.

Due to collective mindsets Koreans use pronouns in plural form, such as "we," "our," and "us" instead of "I," "my," and "me." Koreans say, "our mother," "our house," "our school," and "our country," while Americans will say, "my mother," "my house," "my school," and "my country." By the same token Koreans rarely use the first personal pronoun in daily conversation due to their community consciousness and cohesiveness (Poitras 1977:14). Having corporate ways of thinking, Koreans address strangers who are unrelated to them as if they were related. They call senior citizens, "grandma" or "grandpa." The middle aged they will call "aunt" or "uncle," and the young they will call, "sister" or "brother." Cousins are also called sister or brother. Also Korean college, high school and junior high school students will address their senior class members as "older brother" or "older sister." And they like to do activities together as a group rather than alone.

Because of this corporative identity pervasive throughout the society, we can say that the Korean distinction of self and other is unclear.

When a group of Koreans goes to a restaurant, they tend to eat the same selection of food out of a natural habit of maintaining a sense of harmony. When a husband and wife receive a wedding invitation, either one can go as a representative of the whole family. By the same token if a serious accident happens in a school excursion, the president will resign on behalf of the school. The head of a company or department always bears ultimate responsibility for company accidents or trouble caused by his subordinates that affect others. Since Confucian teaching places emphasis on group harmony and sacrifice for the group, the consciousness of the individual self is subjugated and diffused into group consciousness. The group self demands obedience and sacrifice of the individual self.

Serious problems occur when families move to America: children who receive egalitarian and individualistic input in education conflict with parents who only know the corporate Korean way to raise children. This relational problem between the first and second generations of immigrant families has far reaching implications for the church and society among the immigrants and leads us to the conflicting themes of relationship.

America: Individualism

Noting how individualism arises out of the transition from tribal to class society, Kearney states, "In the Western world it becomes even more prevalent with the decline of kin-based agrarian communities that occurred during the gradual transition from feudalism to capitalism" (1984:75–76). Robert Bellah comments on American individualism:

> American cultural traditions define personality, achievement, and the purpose of human life in ways that leave the individual suspended in glorious, but terrifying isolation. These are limitations of our culture, of the categories and ways of thinking we have inherited (1985:6).

The American self is grounded in individualism with "a belief in the inherent dignity and, indeed, sacredness of the human person" (Bellah, et al. 334). There are different phases of forming individualism and various approaches to studying it. Bellah classifies American individualism into Biblical, republican, utilitarian, and expressive individualism, while Herbert Hoover defines individualism with philosophic, economic, political, and spiritual bases (Morey-Gaines 1979:63).

Morey-Gaines investigates individualism through the symbolic approaches of adamic, material, and rugged individualism. Bercovitch illustrates how American individualism has its roots in Puritanism and how the Puritan concept of self produced an unintended narcissism, which paved the way to later American individualism (1975:24–25). The Puritans were first of all forced by their environmental circumstances to be self-reliant in daily living and survival. Second, their work ethic demanded that they stand on their own feet, work hard to gain wealth, and be good stewards of the wealth earned. Bercovitch observes "the colonial Puritan myth linked self and social assertion in a way that lent special support to the American Way" (1975:185).

Tocqueville saw the great traditions of individualism in the writings of Winthrop, Jefferson, and Benjamin Franklin. Franklin described individualism in his time:

> Our fathers only knew about egoism…. Individualism is a calm and considered feeling which disposes each citizen to isolate himself from the mass of his fellows and withdraw into the circle of family and friends; with this little society formed to his taste, he gladly leaves the greater society to look after itself (quoted in Bellah, et al. 37).

Hoover expressed this in the description of frontier life of the American pioneer: "the American pioneer is the epic expression of…individualism, and pioneer spirit is the response to the challenge of opportunity, to the challenge of nature, to the challenge of life, to the call of the frontier" (quoted in Morey-Gaines 64). Moving west demanded that one leave familiar people and places to confront a new land and new (often dangerous) people, while forging a new life. In addition to lending itself to cooperativeness with other pioneers, this situation simultaneously, and even more strongly, lent itself to the development of a self-reliant life.

This American individualism migrated west with the pioneers, where it stressed a manhood of self-sufficiency, toughness, violence, and ingenuity in the western hero. The frontier entrepreneur created the image of an individual who was a self-redemptive pioneer of opportunity, freedom, progress and equality (Morey-Gaines 142). Western individualism expanded toward agricultural communities in the interior of the continent in places where husbandmen, farmers, owners of the plantations, and slaves were isolated by their environments and struggled against nature, wild animals, native American Indians, and personal relationships with others. The idea of "group" in isolated rural individualism was primarily based on one's family.

The period of rapid westward expansion and industrial growth was followed by the Civil War and later the entry of the United States unto World War I. Through the growth of industrialism, the capitalistic "gospel of wealth" (work hard, secure wealth, and distribute it to the poor) was proclaimed with the doctrine of the free individual and freedom of action in the economic sphere. It implied individual freedom as well as self-responsibility. Laissez-faire ideology promoted both this gospel of wealth and individualism at the end of the century when Darwin's evolutionary theory (which detached people from God and the supernatural) was influential in putting new scientific power in people's hands. American individualism had the support of the best intellectuals.

Self-reliance is the value system of American self-identity, which gives meaning to the self and is proved by leaving home and being independent from one's family. Self-reliance means being separated from family and being self-supporting, standing on one's own feet in life. When a Korean finds American high school students making money by working at a restaurant and many college students supporting themselves by working, he may be very surprised. Worse than that, when he hears that an American is supposed to leave home at the age of eighteen, for the sake of self-reliance, he may be shocked. This is unimaginable in Korean culture, unless due to special circumstances. A Korean is generally supported by parents until he completes his college education. No one leaves home under the guise of freedom or self-reliance. Such an act is considered disloyal to the family and improper for a dutiful son. The self-reliant American leaves not only home but usually the church as well, which means one may not continue to attend the parents' church but will choose one's own church to belong to in order to exercise one's autonomy.

In the same way that people think and live individualistically, their families also tend to be individualistic. Thus, the pervasiveness of nuclear families is an inevitable consequence of individualistic society. Family members themselves are taught to be independent and in adulthood are considered equal in relationship. "They go their way, and I go my own way" is often said of other members in a family. Even children learn to claim independence and equality rather than total obedience while growing up. In Korea even when a sixty-year-old man goes out, his eighty-year-old mother will warn him to cross the street carefully. Children are always expected to be obedient to parents, whether they are ten or sixty years old; there is no equality or individualism. "Individualism" has a negative connotation in Korea as being non-cooperative and detrimental to the vertically oriented collective society.

One reason Americans have so many Nobel prize winners and so many scientific, mechanical and technological inventions compared to Asian countries is because the individual is encouraged to forge ahead into new ideas, to be creative, to express himself, rather than to conform to the group or to the traditions of what has been done in the past. People learn to form their habits of thinking largely independent from others.

Therefore, modern individualism declares self as "the only or main form of reality" (Robert Coles quoted in Bellah, et al. 143). It is no wonder that in America one can find a magazine entitled Self, in which the well-being of the individual is the main concern. The entire judicial system is designed to protect the rights of individuals, often in defiance of the greater society's interests. For example, the American Civil Liberties Union specialized in individual complaints against actions or conditions prevalent among others in a society they must share. Out of the idea of self come many different terms, such as "self seeking," "self esteem," "self improvement," "self satisfaction," "self acceptance," and "self actualization." This language of self deeply reflects American individualism. Bellah illustrates this individualism in its more extreme form as can be seen by a Californian:

> By and large, the rule of thumb here is that if I've got the money, honey, you can do your thing as long as it doesn't destroy someone else's property, or interrupt their sleep, or bother their privacy, then that's fine. If you want to go in your house and smoke marijuana and shoot dope and get all screwed up, that's your business, but don't bring that out on the street, don't expose my children to it, just do your thing. That works out kind of neat (1985:7).

This degree of individualism may be argued to breed loneliness, social anomie, license of freedom, and amoral relationships with one's self and with others.

In Korean culture it is a must for parents to discipline their children with a rod even in high school, but not in America. A rather extreme case in point will illustrate this. One Korean high school student became pregnant by sexual misconduct. The mother was angry and scolded her; the daughter reacted, claiming it was her freedom. The mother slapped her daughter's cheek, and the daughter reported her mother to the police. As a result the mother was taken to jail for three months. After her release the mother took her daughter and returned to Korea. After eight months of residing in Korea, the daughter was changed into an obedient Korean girl, and the whole family sold their property in America and moved permanently back to Korea.

Through the processes of modernization, the ethics of individualism have greatly changed since Tocqueville and Franklin. One of the detrimental factors facing the Korean immigrant family is the inability of Korean parents and children to accommodate the positive side of individualism. Coming from a group oriented tradition, Koreans are grappling with the realities of individualism.

Relationship

Concepts of relationship are a fourth area of fundamental difference between Korean and American worldviews. One is essentially hierarchical, the other, egalitarian.

Korea: Vertical

The Confucian ideology adopted by the Yi Dynasty promoted "ruler-subject" values, such as loyalty to one's ruler, filial piety to one's parents, a hierarchical relationship and subordination of wife to husband, younger friend to older friend, and younger brother to elder brother (Chung 1982:100). These values all maintain vertical relationships, which set the roles of ruler and subject through all of society.

Confucius' five virtues (benevolent love, righteousness, propriety, wisdom, and faithfulness) and five relationships (sovereign and subject, father and son, husband and wife, elder and younger, and friend and friend) were postulated as fundamental ethical principles, and each was characterized by intimacy, righteousness, obedience, and faithfulness.

Proper worship of heaven, nature and ancestors was vital to maintaining the harmony of the cosmic order. The principle of these relationships, which was the highest human and social value, embodied self, society, state, and cosmic order. The Yi Dynasty established Neo-Confucianism as the ideological basis for social order, land reform, and a central hierarchical state of king, chiefs, ministers, high officials, gentlemen-scholars, and commoners, along with the duties that governed the hierarchical relationships.

According to this concept complete subordination of a son to his father and a wife to her husband were absolute expectations. Violating this order was considered disruptive rebellion against the laws of nature and norms of the society and, therefore, was strictly sanctioned (Hei Chu Kim 1982:94). Absolute subordination was thus a cardinal virtue and the predominant moral code of filial piety.

The strong emphasis on filial piety developed patriarchal, extended and traditional family systems that gave power to parents, husbands and sons. Sons were regarded as being more important than daughters, because sons inherited the lineage, prestige, and fortunes of the family, and because they carried out the duties of ancestral worship. It was taught that when people observe these principles, society carries on harmoniously and in order. But this system has, over five hundred years, also produced a bureaucratic hierarchy in Korean society.

Thus, when two Koreans encounter each other, they must clarify the age, family name, year of graduation, and from what school the other graduated in order to establish who is socially superior. Due to this vertical concept of relationships, the Korean language uses five levels of respective verb endings: for kings, nobility, elders, friends, and those younger or inferior. In contemporary society the language for kings has disappeared, yet Christians use that when speaking to God in prayer. The rest of the formal respective endings are still used.

By contrast, in America the word "fair" became the crown of human relationships. "That's not fair" is one of the most common phrases Korean children learn from their school friends. It functions as a verbal scale to weigh the equality of individuals.

America: Egalitarianism

In their concept of self, Americans are not bound by family or other group affiliations; they are given equal chance to make the best of themselves, and though equality of opportunity is essential, inequality is a natural result.

One of the most outstanding figures of American democracy is Thomas Jefferson, who began the Declaration of Independence with the words, "All men are created equal." By equality he meant "fundamental political equality" (Bellah, et al. 1985:30). Also in his inaugural address Jefferson stressed, "equal and exact justice to all men, of whatever state or persuasion, religious or political" (Bellah, et al. 1985:31). To be sure, there was social and economic inequality, particularly manifest in slavery, racial prejudice and the gap between the rich and poor, yet people forged a way of thinking that asserted, and would later realize, natural rights, liberty, and pursuit of happiness as expressed by Jefferson in the Declaration of Independence.

Since Jefferson's theory of free individual rights and liberty became the bulwark of American democracy, "it was his pride that every American was equal before the Law, that no one—not even the highest official—was immune" (Henry Commager 1950:20).

When Hector St. John de Crèvecoeur, a French settler in New York who issued a small pamphlet in 1782 *titled Letters from an American Farmer*, depicting America as a land of opportunity, egalitarianism had already developed. Crèvecoeur clearly describes: "From nothing to start into being; from a servant to the rank of a master; from being the slave to some despotic prince, to become a free man, invested with lands, to which every municipal blessing is annexed! What a change indeed! It is in consequence of that change he becomes an American" (1981:83).

Crèvecoeur stressed equal opportunity in this nation of immigrants, seeing it as liberation from the European feudalistic mentality. Crèvecoeur also wrote, "Here the rewards of his industry follow with equal steps the progress of his labour; his labour is founded on the basis of nature, self interest; can it want a stronger allurement?" (1981:70). Crèvecoeur considered the nature and results of one's labor to be the rewards of one's labor. Having focused on visible equality of his contemporaries, he was unable to foresee the coming age of capitalistic bureaucratic institutionalization in a socially and politically egalitarian structure.

Despite these developments, Commager was still able to say, "Throughout the nineteenth century, the sense of equality permeated the American's life and thought, his conduct, work, and play, his language, and literature, his religion and his politics, and it conditioned al the relationships of his life" (1950:13).

Commager argued that equality was not primarily political; rather it was social, cultural, and psychological, and was chiefly the absence of class distinction rather than triumph over them. Wherever men and women gathered they met on the bases of equality (1950:13–14). Commager indicates that Americans tend to be disparaging toward hierarchical authority, bureaucrats and disciplinarians. For example, Americans often call each other by first names to express "closeness" in relationship even if the other party is older or higher in social relationship or has authority over them. "This is my buddy," is the token of intimate relations, a concept that would be impolite in a society oriented around vertical relationships, like Korea.

In English the word "you" is used for all people, while Korean uses four different levels of politeness. Americans will use Mr. or Mrs. As a respectful prefix, while to a Korean the same Mr. and Mrs. or Miss is a common, rather humiliating prefix, because of their title-oriented vertical relationships.

A Korean will be called by a title expressing his social status, for example, "teacher, pastor, doctor, section chief." Someone who does not have official status will be recognized as a "teacher," and a person who runs a small business will be called "president." If a person is unemployed, he will be called by the title of his former occupation. In Korean culture equal friends are usually limited to old classmates, otherwise everyone else is superior or inferior in relationship. If a sister is one year older than her younger sister, the younger will call the older "older sister," rather than by her first name. Their relationship is not equal. Thus, it is difficult for a Korean to understand American egalitarian concepts in daily life situations, because Americans have little concept of the vertical in human relations, while Koreans were born and raised in it.

In American churches committees are the servants who run the church. Decisions are usually made by committees. But in Korea the pastor is supra-committee. If a pastor needs something for the benefit of church, the committee is compliant and flexible. This is because the church respects that pastor's authority and is run on a vertical axis rather than a horizontal democratic line. An American pastor is expected to be a "nice guy," while a Korean pastor must be spiritually powerful. American church members often treat their pastors as friends or brothers rather than as spiritual leaders. And, consequently, members tend to prefer therapy and counseling (in which they can express themselves) as opposed to directive discipline.

Since an individual is entitled to claim rights, fairness and nonconformity (which result in isolation), the power of the individual is the ballot, and the government is administered by that voting power. Since governmental offices are determined by vote, church pastors and leaders are also chosen by ballot, and church decisions are made by vote. Since each ballot is equal, each individual has equal power. Administration of the church in America naturally reflects this fundamental pattern of democracy.

Acculturation

I often encounter the question from American pastoral colleagues, "Why don't Koreans become like Americans rather than insisting on maintaining Korea culture after they have come to live in America?" Sociologists and cultural anthropologists refer to this problem as one of "acculturation" or "assimilation." Sometimes these two terms are used to mean the same thing: sociologists prefer the term "assimilation" while anthropologists prefer "acculturation" (Milton Gordon 1964:61).

"Acculturation" was defined in 1936 by the Social Science Research Council's Subcommittee on Acculturation, engaging such anthropologists as Robert Redfield, Ralph Linton and Melville J. Herskovits. Acculturation, they stated:

> comprehends those phenomena which result when groups of individuals having different cultures come into continuous first-hand contact, with subsequent changes in the original cultural patterns of either or both groups ("Memorandum" for the study of Acculturation, *American Anthropologist* 1936:149).

In this statement the changes are said to be in terms of cultural patterns rather than social relationships or the degree or nature of structural integration of the two groups. Certainly a change in cultural patterns may take place, yet the deep level of Korean social relationships may remain unchanged.

Robert E. Park defines "assimilation" as: "the process or processes by which peoples of diverse racial origins and different cultural heritages, occupying a common territory, achieve a cultural solidarity sufficient at least to sustain a national existence" (1930:281). According to this definition a Korean and his family can achieve cultural solidarity with Americans. There is little possibility the Korean culture will rapidly and entirely change, yet it might change gradually by the pull of the social structural system. Park adds:

> In the United States an immigrant is ordinarily considered assimilated as soon as he has acquired the language and the social ritual of the native community and can participate without

encountering prejudice in the common life, economic and political. The common sense view of the matter is than an immigrant is assimilated as soon as he has shown that he can "get on in the country." This implies among other things that in all the ordinary affairs of life he is able to find a place in the community on the basis of his individual merits without invidious or qualifying reference to his racial origin or to his cultural inheritance (1930:281).

Park did not make distinctions between prejudice (an attitude of the heart) and discrimination (the result of that attitude). Until the immigrant can participate in the host community without encountering prejudicial attitudes and discriminatory acts, assimilation has not occurred. If a Korean can work in an Anglo community without encountering prejudicial attitudes or discriminatory behavior, that person is regarded to have assimilated. Different sociologists have produced an array of assimilation theories, yet Gordon generalizes as follows: "When structural assimilation has occurred, either simultaneously with or subsequent to acculturation, all of the other types of assimilation will naturally follow" (1964:81). He further points out that acculturation does not lead to structural assimilation, while structural assimilation will produce cultural assimilation or acculturation (1964:81).

George Foster saw the somewhat universal motivations of cultural change as "the desire for prestige, or for economic gain, and the wish to comply with friendship obligations" (1973:152). But for Koreans it may not be applicable since Koreatown is the center of most social and economic activities. Thus a complete cultural and structural assimilation occurs slowly over several generations, after which ethnic identity and distinctive values disappear.

Gordon firmly stated, "if marital assimilation, an inevitable by-product of structural assimilation, takes place fully, the minority group loses its ethnic identity in the larger host or core society, and identificational assimilation takes place" (1964:80). If a Korean woman marries an American, she no longer faces prejudice or discrimination by Americans, and the children of this intermarriage are identified as Americans. Gordon believes that structural assimilation is gradually followed by more pervasive acculturation (1964:81). If a Korean marries an American, acculturation inevitably occurs. But Koreans are not in favor of intermarriage, and as a result assimilation does not take place as the assimilationist would expect. For example, a Korean seminarian who was raised in America and married to an American applied for the position of youth pastor in many Korean churches. Even though there was a great need for Korean youth workers in Korean-American churches, this couple was repeatedly turned down because of their cross-cultural marriage.

Theories of Assimilation

Gordon presents three central ideological tendencies: Anglo-conformity, the "melting pot, and cultural pluralism" (1964:85). Gordon defines the theories as follows: Anglo-Conformity Theory is "the complete renunciation of the immigrants' ancestral culture in favor of the behavior and values of the Anglo-Saxon core group" (1964:85). The Melting Pot Theory is "a biological merger of the Anglo-Saxon people with other immigrant groups and a blending of their respective cultures into a new indigenous American type" (1964:85). The Cultural Pluralism Theory is "the preservation of the communal life and significant portion of the culture of the later immigrant groups within the context of the American citizenship and political and economic integration into American society" (1964:85).

Anglo-Conformity. This theory was labeled by S.G. and M.W. Cole (1954), and according to Gordon, Anglo-Conformity is the "most prevalent ideology of assimilation in America throughout the nation's history" (1964:89). This theory assumes that any group of immigrants should break away from their native culture in order to "assimilate and amalgamate" into the general population of Americans, implanting in their children an "Anglo-Saxon conception of righteousness, law and order" (1964:98). Anglo-Conformity theory assumes that all immigrant groups will adopt Anglo-Saxon cultural patterns at the deprivation of their own linguistic and national identity. This theory postulates that Koreans can and should adopt Anglo-Saxon cultural patterns.

The Melting Pot. The concept of the melting pot can be first identified in Crèvecoeur's Letters from an American Farmer. The central theme of the booklet reveals how individuals of all nations are melted into a new race of people under a new mode of life and new government and new ranks. He pointed out "a mixture of English, Scotch, Irish, French, Dutch, Germans, and Swedes," and continued, "From this promiscuous breed the race now called American has arisen" (Crèvecoeur 1981:51).

This idea was developed further by Ralph Waldo Emerson and Frederick Jackson Turner. Turner presented a paper entitled, "The Significance of the Frontier in American History," to the American and democracy are shaped not by dominant European heritage but by the western frontier, which acted as solvent and melting pot for national heritage (Gordon 117–119). This idea has been called Turner's "frontier melting pot theory."

The people Turner referred to were contemporary immigrants from countries of northwestern Europe, the so-called "old immigration" of people having a similar culture and physical appearance (Gordon 1964:119). Melting was by intermarriage through which the combining of gene pools led to a complete mixture. This idea had many proponents and led to a single melting pot theory.

Israel Zangwill's drama of 1908, *The Melting Pot*, popularized the term. It describes America as "God's crucible, the great Melting Pot where all the races of Europe are melting and re-forming!" In the play it is said, "Germans and Frenchmen, Irishmen and Englishmen, Jews and Russians—into the Crucible with you all! God is making the American" (Gordon 1964:120).

In 1914 the Ford Motor Company started the Ford English School to homogenize immigrant workers and displayed a "Ford Melting Pot" at the graduation ceremony, through which immigrant workers would walk and come out "American" (C. Peter Wagner 1979:45–46). The implication of the "Ford Melting Pot" was an assimilation of all ethnic groups into a new blend, the American. This melting pot idea was predominant in political, social and even in religious institutions. Prior to 1970 this postulate assumed that "nuisance" ethnicity would be melted by the "heat of the melting pot" (Wagner 1979:46).

This assumption has encountered difficulties in reconciling the reality of an undissolving Eastern European influx into the southeastern U.S.A. during the last two decades of the 19th century, the so called "new immigrants, who were culturally different from the old immigrants. Ruby Jo Reeves Kennedy researched intermarriage and declared it a "triple melting pot" when religious differences are involved (1944:331–9). Later, theologian Will Herberg used the thesis of the triple melting pot and wrote an analysis of religious trends in American society, Protestant, Catholic and Jew (Gordon 1964:124). Out of this multiple melting pot and new idea appeared.

Cultural Pluralism. The previous two theories may have been applicable in varying degrees to immigrants of similar cultural backgrounds. But since the 1970's the third wave of immigrants, this time from Southeast Asia (Koreans, Taiwanese, Chinese, Vietnamese, Cambodians, and Filipinos), has proven these previous assimilation theories to be inapplicable to culturally distant immigrant groups. The different ethnic groups have formed their own enclaves; in Los Angeles for example, Korea Town, Little Tokyo, and Chinatown. They maintain their own national, cultural, and linguistic traits and heritages rather than blending into a single, double or triple melting pot or a "transmuting pot" (George R. Stewart 1954:23). I agree with Andrew Greeley's usage of "the stew pot" (quoted in Wagner 1979:51) or Gordon's term, "a multiple melting pot" (1964:131) to describe cultural pluralism.

We can see then how cultural assimilation of Koreans will not easily occur, either by the American melting pot or by absorbing cultural patterns as assimilationists allude. Likewise, structural assimilation of the Koreans cannot take place as the melting pot theory assumes, because of the great chasm of linguistic, cultural and worldview differences.

Gordon's pluralistic model sees America as a nation that maintains diverse groups within a national unity (1964:158). Therefore, ethnic groups should no more be thought of as un-Americanized and needing to be assimilated. Because Koreans have a much greater cultural distance from the mainstream Anglo-American populace than do the "old immigrants" from Europe, it is unrealistic to expect them to assimilate into American cultural behavior in the first and second generations. Fundamental to this distance is the difference we have observed in worldview between Koreans and Americans.

Illustrations of Acculturation in the 1.5 Generation

Wagner categorizes different social behaviors of individuals within ethnic groups in establishing the nature of their ethnic identity. Korean immigrants working in Korean Town can be identified as "nuclear ethnic." Those who live partly within the Korean community and partly outside of the Korean community (e.g., their job or school is outside) would be called "fellow traveler ethnic." Those who do not identify with being Korean yet participate in special events would be called "marginal ethnic." Those who completely disconnect themselves from their Korean identity are "alienated ethnics," who in turn would become "affiliate ethnics" into another ethnic group (Wagner 1983:9).

First and 1.5-generation Koreans will rarely be alienated or affiliate ethnics. First-generation Koreans generally remain nuclear ethnics. 1.5-generation Koreans almost invariable find themselves as fellow traveler. They will also be marginal for a time, but very frequently turn back to affiliate more thoroughly with the Korean community. Second- and third-generation Koreans are still so few that it is difficult to accurately say which direction they will take. To illustrate the process and degree of acculturation, I will describe several examples of 1.5-generation Korean immigrants in my own ministry.

Priscilla is a college student who came to the U.S.A. at the age of three and only speaks English. Her parents are not able to communicate in English, therefore, they speak to her in Korean and she responds in English. She speaks Korean with an English accent. But in college she realized that she did not fit in with the Anglo-American groups. She sought her identity and discovered the need of learning Korean language and culture. Now she speaks pretty good Korean. She eats Korean food. She feels closer to Koreans than Americans in heart, yet she doesn't really know Korean culture. And she thinks the way Americans do because she learned to think under American teachers.

Bob came to America when he was three months old. He is an engineering student. He eats Korean food and is used to speaking English. He speaks English at home. His father speaks English, and his mother understands it but speaks Korean to him. He was insecure because he did not know where he belonged. When he joined a Korean Bible Study group, he felt better because he felt accepted by the Korean-speaking group. Then he decided to learn Korean. Now he is deeply involved in a campus ministry working with English-speaking Koreans of the second generation.

Debbie is a college student born in the U.S.A. whose parents speak English at home. She struggled to search out her identity through junior high to college period. She found that she belonged to the Korean community and she began to pick up Korean words and phrases by interacting with Korean friends on campus. Now she speaks fluent Korean. Her father forbade her to marry a non-Korean. She has been called minister to second-generation Koreans who are suffering through the same things.

James was three years old when he came to the U.S.A. He is completely bilingual. He speaks Korean at home. He teaches Sunday school as his ministry, and works at the University of Southern California as a lab technician. He struggled to find his identity, but now he knows himself as a second-generation Korean-American.

Jay was born in the U.S.A. into a dysfunctional non-Christian home. He was raised by a black family in the neighborhood. He talked, acted, and thought like a black because he identified with blacks. He did not have Korean identity. He is the rare Korean who lost his Korean identity completely, yet he eats *kimchi* and understands Korean. His mother speaks Korean to him, and he responds in English to her, while his father communicates with him in English. Jay and was a member of a black gang and was sentenced to jail.

Gee came to America when she was six years old now she is in the eleventh grade at a senior high school. She speaks Korean to her grand parents and parents but to her brothers, sisters and friends she communicates in English. Despite this she cooks and eats Korean food, and her best friends are all Koreans.

Steve came to America at age six and is a college student of twenty-one. Yet he speaks Korean as his first language and eats Korean food. He can't eat a meal without *kimchi*, and he does not think a man can cook or prepare food. He thinks the way the Koreans do.

Esther came to the United States when she had just turned ten. She grew up in Korea Town speaking Korean at home and English at school. She has now graduated from college and is studying at a graduate school. She works at California Institute of Technology as a lab technician and is bilingual. She eats American food as well as Korean food. She has been called into Christian work and is working for the second-generation Koreans at a Korean Church of the Nazarene.

The above cases are very common as Korean American cultural and linguistic descriptions. These cases are of 1.5-generation Korean immigrants. Culturally and linguistically these people are close to being American yet assimilation has not occurred to full degree. The children of these people will be called second-generation Korean-Americans.

We have discussed the deep level realities of Korean culture and worldview themes, comparing them with those of Americans. We have attempted to compare five major areas of worldview to find differences and areas of acculturation so as to understand the felt needs of Korean hearts and minds in order to design a fitting contextualization for Koreans. We will now begin to examine the needs and problems of the Korean Church of the Nazarene in America in order to search for appropriate areas of contextualization.

Chapter 7

THE KOREAN CHURCH OF THE NAZARENE IN THE U.S.A.

Korean immigration began early in the 19th century, but the major influx was from the 1970s. Thus, 90 percent of Korean churches in California were started in the 1970s, Nazarenes among them. As an immigrant church, Koreans faces numerous cultural difficulties, as well as differences in theological and leadership perspectives, when working directly under American leadership.

Immigration

The history of Korean immigration to American began in 1903 when sugar cane laborers arrived in Hawaii. The Koreans in the U.S.A. continued to survive as an insignificant ethnic entity until the Korean War broke out and triggered the second wave of Korean immigration to the States. According to the U.S. Immigration and Naturalization Service, 1400 orphans and wives of servicemen came to this country in the 1950s.

The influx of Korean immigration started with the passage of the Immigration and Naturalization Act in 1965. Immigration and Naturalization Service reports show that between 1965 and 1980 a total of 299,000 Koreans immigrated into the United States. The

1980 U.S. Census found 354,529 Koreans in this country (Yu, Phillips and Yang 1982:1).

Koreans in the Los Angeles area, the greatest Korean population outside Korea, are estimated at 50,000 (Wagner's plenary address to the National Convocation on Evangelizing Ethnic America, Houston, Texas, April 1985). Los Angeles has become the largest port of entry for Korean immigrants and home to the largest Korean community outside Korea.

The Korean population in Los Angeles increased visibly during the 70s and 80s as Koreans opened small businesses, aggressively penetrating city ghettos as well as posh white neighborhoods. They cleaned and revived decayed sections of the city, establishing new business communities and shopping facilities mainly in an area now known as Koreatown.

The Korean Christian community has rapidly increased in numbers, and Korean churches multiplied like bamboo shoots after rain. The predominant denominations are Presbyterian, Methodist, Holiness, Assembly of God, and Baptist. After two decades the count is at about 600 churches in Southern California.

A Brief History of the Korean Church of the Nazarene in Southern California

At the time of this writing, there are nine Korean Churches of the Nazarene in southern California. The Los Angeles District has five Korean churches: Los Angeles Korean, Los Angeles First Korean (Praise Church), Glendale Korean Community, San Luis Korean, and Alhambra Korean (Kamsa Church). The Anaheim District has two Korean Churches, Anaheim Korean, and Cerritos Korean, while the Chula Vista Korean Church belongs to the Southern California District.

The first Korean church was The Los Angeles Korean Church of the Nazarene, planted by Soo-Goon Hearn, a Conservative Baptist, on February 14, 1971. He pioneered a Korean congregation in the facilities of the English speaking L.A. First Church of the Nazarene with fourteen people as charter members, including his wife and two children. According to Hearn it was the 29th Korean church in the Los Angeles basin, and it increased to

118

150 people, including youth, within four years. Hearn joined the Church of the Nazarene in 1971.

Some Koreans who secured stable jobs or businesses began to move out of downtown to the suburban Hacienda Heights area. Hearn and some of his church members purchased houses and decided to relocate the church there, expecting future church growth in this newly developing Korean community. But due to the long distance from the former location, the church decreased forty-five percent after relocating. Following that, the church split over doctrinal disagreements between the pastor and members who had been Presbyterian. The church has never regained what it had in its first five years of growth. Currently his membership is seventy-nine including children and youth; Sunday worship is held in the Hacienda Heights Church of the Nazarene (Hearn 1989).

The second church in Los Angeles was started by David Kwon in 1975 and closed in 1986 after eleven years of little or no growth. He left the denomination. In 1980, Bong Whan Lee, a former District Superintendent in Korea started the third congregation in Westchester, but this also closed after two-years' struggle. The Anglo pastor and congregation were fully supportive, but the Korean demographic distribution was a disadvantage for the growth of this church.

In 1981 the late Young Joon Lee planted the Chula Vista Korean Nazarene Church near San Diego and pastored for eight years until he passed away in 1989. Currently Young Suk Kang, who came from Korea in 1990, is pastoring and struggling to lead this church with its twenty people to growth. At the same time the fifth congregation was gathered by Kyung Hak Yoon in Santa Monica, but ceased to meet about two years later in 1982.

Cho Moon Kyung planted the Anaheim Korean Church with his wife and two children on January 14, 1982. This church has showed gradual growth. The church now has its own facility and at present attendance averages 230, including children; they have thirty deacons and one elder. This is presently the largest Korean Church of the Nazarene in Southern California.

I myself started the sixth congregation of the Korean Church of the Nazarene with five founding members in the Glendale First Church of the Nazarene on July 30, 1983. Six months later I relocated the congregation to the Los Angeles First Church of the

Nazarene by invitation of its church board. In 1985 Sung Dae Kim, took over the ministry and has pastored the congregation until the present time. The congregation is composed of recently arrived Korean immigrants who are, as yet, unsettled. They have strong Korean cultural traits and are not acculturated to America.

This Korean congregation encounters frequent cultural conflicts with the host English speaking congregation. Ron Benefiel, the English-speaking pastor, has endeavored to understand and reconcile the situation, and Sung Dae Kim has also been striving to understand American worldview and culture. This church had been growing well, when a sudden split in 1987 resulted in two-thirds of the congregation leaving. The problem was the absence of leadership for women's ministry. Currently they maintain one hundred people, including children. The church has a strong children's ministry through Sunday school and children's small group meetings, but these have caused endless culturally related problems between the English- and Korean-speaking members.

Jae Don Yang, a Presbyterian minister who wanted to become Nazarene, started the seventh church, which was with the Hollywood Church of the Nazarene. But due to cultural clashes the English-speaking congregation asked them to leave in 1982. He relocated the congregation to Echo Park Spanish-speaking Church of the Nazarene. Later he left the Church of the Nazarene.

The eighth congregation was brought into the church of the Nazarene by Young Hoon Lee, a former Church of God (Anderson) pastor. He joined the Church of the Nazarene and came to the Glendale First Church of the Nazarene in June 1984 with one hundred members, including children. But he has been scarcely involved in any Church of the Nazarene District activities. At present his membership is 149 (1991).

The ninth congregation was aborted before formation. In 1987 I attempted to pioneer a new congregation in the Northridge Community Church of Nazarene. Some of the deacons strongly desired to start an ethnic ministry to reach the new neighbors, but unfortunately, the senior pastor was disinterested from the start. Consequently, it became impossible to launch a Korean congregation of the Church of the Nazarene there.

Tenth, Joshua Kim, a Presbyterian minister, started a congregation in the Walnut Church of the Nazarene in March 1988, but it closed in December that year. They had difficulties with the Anglo congregation and pastor over leadership and financial matters.

The eleventh effort was, in January 1988 when Joo Kye Young, a former Presbyterian ordained minister, founded a Korean church at Bellflower Church of the Nazarene in the city of Bellflower. Six months later the Anglo church sold the property and relocated to the present newly constructed facility in Cerritos. Joo's congregation moved in with them and has thirty members, with Sunday worship attendance at about twenty. They have seven deacons and one *kwonsa* (a rank between deacon and elder).

In addition to these eleven church planting efforts, there were two college campus Bible class fellowships that later became 1.5-generation Korean churches. One was started by Bong Soo Kim, a Korean Professor of aeronautical engineering of California Polytechnic University, San Luis Obispo in 1987 and joined the San Luis Obispo Church of the Nazarene. The other was at San Antonio Community College in the City of Walnut.

In 1988 Bong Soo Kim was transferred to Lincoln, Nebraska and the student church was left without a pastor. Since I was a Korean coordinator I pastored them by driving up there once a month and having them down to Alhambra once a month. In 1990 I could not continue ministering, and the young church was left without a pastor. With no pool of pastors, the church accepted a Korean Baptist minister who recently came from Korea, but he soon left.

In 1990 I established a Bible class fellowship at Mt. San Antonio City College campus. Since there were sixteen new converts, I tried to secure a church facility and start a 1.5-generation church in facilities in Hacienda and Walnut area, yet I was not successful. As a result, I brought a couple of new converts to the Alhambra Church of the Nazarene, where Fletcher Tink was pastoring. With his encouragement and support I started a new ministry that became the Kamsa Church of the Nazarene.

Altogether thirteen new ministries were pioneered in Southern California. In the Los Angeles District there were nine churches pioneered from 1970 to 1992, but only four churches survive today.

The District Superintendent, Paul Benefiel, employed the so-called "multi-congregational structure" to reach various ethnic groups and to share facilities in order to build up ethnic churches as part of English speaking churches. It is an ideal ecclesiastical structure in L.A.'s multi-ethnic demography.

The definitions of the multi-congregational model are the following: A Bible class ministry is the beginning stage for multi-congregational evolution. Sunday school classes or Bible studies are conducted in another language. The local church sponsors this class and supports it financially, if necessary. Department ministry is more extensive than the first stage of development, since it provides for worship services and fellowship opportunities in another language ("Guidelines For Multi-Congregational Ministries of L.A. District," 1989).

In the 1989 *Manual* there are similar rules to the above guidelines regarding administrational integration (59–60). This structure is applied more in terms of sharing buildings than ministries.

Problems Faced by the Korean Nazarene Church

Being an immigrant church, the Korean Church of the Nazarene in California faces several problems. These problems are directly related to contextualization. The problems are not only related to the family but also to the church and community as a whole. Therefore, we will discuss the problems for a better understanding of the context.

Interpersonal—Relational
Like other immigrants in the United States, Koreans are in a situation of encountering cultural, racial, linguistic, and social barriers. They are residing in an entirely different life situation from those in Korea. Accordingly, this situation induces heavy stress, insecurity, frustration, and generates cultural shock, family crises, anxiety, and various fears of living with cultural barriers. They experience a lack of acceptance resulting from racial discrimination of the host nationals. In turn, their self-identity is

damaged, which cause family crises and loss of self-esteem and credibility. This brings frequent but unavoidable inner friction within the Korean community.

The expected harmony of the immigrant's family life becomes largely unbalanced in the struggle for assimilation into the new culture. These factors simply exemplify the complex problems and needs among Korean immigrants.

Intergenerational—Communicational

A different set of problems arises with the second generation, who learn to be Americans with a basic sense of independence and egalitarianism. Since the children use English every day, English becomes their primary language of communication. Sooner or later the parents reach the point where they are unable to communicate on a deep level with their own children.

This results in inter-generational communication problems. In fact, it is an international problem within a home. In addition, dislocation of social status as immigrants, and difficulty of communicating and securing a job beyond the Korean community causes discontent and disequilibrium in the family.

Intercultural—Organizational

Coming from a vertical and relational society, Korean immigrants struggle to settle down to a horizontal and individual social structure. The major source of all these problems is rooted in worldview differences. As an outcome of Confucianism, Koreans are deeply imbued with ruler-subject relationship and ancestral veneration. Thus, it is not easy for a Korean to become individualistic, independent, and egalitarian in thought and cultural patterns or behaviors, even though she or he holds a permanent residence card.

The difference between American and Korean culture is much greater than that between American and Mexican or Filipino. Acculturation occurs much more slowly. This can be seen in pastors' responses to a questionnaire I distributed at a November 1986 West Coast regional Korean pastors' fellowship in Anaheim, CA. I asked the following questions:

1. How long have you pastored in the United States?

Of eight who answered, four had pastored here less than five years and four more than ten years.

2. How many deacons and elders do you have in your church?
   Of seven who answered, two had elders; one had three and the other had one. Two pastors had three deacons, and two had six deacons. The other three had ten, four, and thirteen respectively.

3. Do you think the Korean church in the U.S.A. needs ruling elders?
   All nine said yes.

4. What do you think of the limit of thirteen deacons?
   Eight pastors answered, giving the following responses:
   It has practical problems.
   It would be better to be flexible according to the size of a church.
   It would better with no limits.
   If the church expands we need more than thirteen deacons.
   It is too small a number of deacons.
   I think it is better to number deacons according to the membership of the church
   It would be better without limits. What if the church expands?
   It would be good to control the number according to the needs.

   These pastors consistently disagree with the limit on deacons, pointing out that more deacons are called for as the church grows.

5. What do you think of the system of probational membership for Korean converts who drink and smoke?
   Seven pastors answered:
   I feel it is impossible to practice.
   It is not good.
   It is not a favorable system because it is not a big matter for a new convert.

We need to receive them as members.
It should be amended.
It is nothing but a problem.
I feel it is unbiblical, because Jesus received them already.

Again, we see consistent disagreement with the system. Ruling elders and unrestricted numbers of deacons are necessary for the normal functioning of a Korean church. Major barriers to Koreans' conversion are ancestral worship and shamanistic practice, not smoking and drinking. Thus we can say that the pastors' responses revealed their cultural and worldview differences.

The Culture of Nazarene Church Tradition

In order to understand and discuss theological issues between the Korean and American Church of the Nazarene, we must remember the origins and core beliefs of the Nazarenes. The Holiness Movement was the result of a spiritual awakening before the turn of the century in a revival of John Wesley's preaching and teaching of holiness.

The Nazarenes were formed out of those who rejected wild emotions and speaking in unknown tongues. Since the Holiness Movement consisted of those who came out of the Methodist, Congregational, and Presbyterian churches (Smith 1962:28), the constitutions and the general rules were for the American context.

The doctrines essential to Christian life and fellowship were essentially conservative evangelical with a stress on the holiness of God, which they have continued to faithfully believe and practice until the present day. It is appropriate for the people in that historical context as well as of today, but is it relevant to the Koreans who have strong beliefs about demons but know very little about an Almighty God?

General and Special Rules of the
Church of the Nazarene Constitution

The 1985 *Manual* of the Nazarene Church carries exactly the same articles and general rules as did the *Manual* of 1895. The divisions are:

A. Christian life
B. Marriage and divorce and/or dissolution of marriage
C. Abortion
D. Homosexuality
E. Christian stewardship
F. Church officers
G. Amending special rules

The legislative section in the *Manual* of 1911 (and church government section in 1932 and 1989) details that the allowable number of stewards shall be no fewer than three and no more than thirteen.

I submit that if the rules were written by Koreans, we would likely see additional articles such as, Abandoning Ancestral Worship, Abstaining from Shamanistic Practices (counseling with shamen, astrology, fortunetelling, geomancy), and Prohibition of Concubinage.

Divorce and homosexuality are neither acceptable nor as prevalent in Korean culture as in American. Rather, the greatest obstacles to faith are ancestral worship, shamanism, and concubinage, which as we have seen, are deeply rooted in social and familial structures. That means a Korean person's conversion goes through quite different processes. The indication of a Korean's conversion is to quit shamanistic practices and counseling with shamen, geomancers, palm readers, face readers, fortunetellers, and name makers. The American Nazarene rules are important, but are not inclusive of the real issues in Korean conversion.

In 1984 as a pastor of a very new congregation of Korean Church of the Nazarene, I encountered a disturbing problem regarding the reception of new members who drank and smoked. They had already made dramatic changes in their lives by turning away from bad relationships, beliefs, and ways of life, but had not yet made a complete change.

However, according to the *Manual* they were to remain as probational members until they quit the old habits. This is a significant issue in a theology of conversion. Thus, at this point I will briefly discuss the biblical meaning of conversion in order to shed some light on the basic issues of what it means to turn to the true and living God.

Theological Issues

Whatever living standard a people may have, their basic human problem is not social or material but spiritual. Thus, the, basic need is salvation of their souls. Turning from spiritual death to life, a person's conversion is the most significant step of salvation. The understanding of conversion is fundamental to doing theology in context.

Conversion in the Old Testament

Conversion as a change of direction in terms of everyday life implies a new beginning. In the Old Testament, the term *shuv* is used 118 times to describe a change in a person's relationship with God (David John Price 1979:289). *Shuv* is described as being a "return to Yahweh for the sake of reconciliation and restoration of relationship with God" (Price 1979:294). The implication of the verb often carries the meaning of conversion to God—a person's encounter and new relationship with the living God.

William Barclay defines conversion as a turning of the person's mind, heart and life in the direction of God (1964:23). The word *niham* is parallel to *shuv*, yet it is more implicit. *Shuv* is a word for explicit motion while *niham* is one for emotion "to sigh" or "to regret" (Ps.77:2; 90:13; 1 Sam.15:29; Isa.1:24–25; (J.W. Heikkinen 1967:135 cf. Hans Kasdorf 1980:44). According to Christopher Barth returning to God means returning to a covenantal relationship with Yahweh in the Old Testament (1967:310).

A covenantal relationship with the living God demands obedience and loyalty, and when His community failed to keep that obligation it was essential for them to "turn back" to God. Turning back to God's covenant is the primary condition for God's people to repent of their sins of violation or disobedience (Jer.15:19; Neh.1:9; Hos.6:1; Joel 2:12) (Heikkinen 1967:316).

Conversion in the New Testament

In Greek *epistrepho* is parallel to *shuv* in the Old Testament (C. Brown 1975:357). It describes different types of change and turning: "turn around," "turn back," and "bring back." Matthew wrote, "Judas the betrayer having regretted, brought back the thirty pieces of silver" (27:3). Luke wrote, "The Lord turned around, he looked at Peter" (22:61). Mark wrote, "Jesus turned around and rebuked Peter" (8:33). Luke wrote that "he will go on before the Lord…to turn the hearts of the fathers" (Lk.1:17). Peter, reflecting on the Servant Song in Isaiah, urged, "For you were straying like sheep but have returned to the shepherd" (1 Pet.2:25). Paul reminded the Thessalonian church how "they turned to God from idols" (1 Thess.1:1–9).

Epistrepho, "turn," is used for outward change of direction, renewing fellowship and making new contacts in the sense of bringing back, turning back, or turning around. The frequent use of *epistrepho* suggests a new turning to God from man's will, and it means to turn to Christ, through whom we turn to God. The noun *epistrepho* is a turning around in terms of the physical, mental and spiritual sense. It occurs more than thirty-six times in the New Testament. It is the most frequently used noun for the physical, mental or spiritual turn (Acts 3:19; 9:35; 11:21; 14:15; 15:19; 26:18; 26:2).

The basic idea of *epistrepho* and *epistrephein* is that of a turn, a change of direction, a reversal of life (Barclay 1964:22–24). Kasdorf made a clear distinction of the word *epistrepho* as being more external and "motive" rather than "emotive" in its causal function (1980:49).

Metaneo is the New Testament rendition of *niham* and appears thirty-five times in the LXX either as *metaneo* or *metamelomai*, showing similar usage to classical Greek in distinguishing these two words. *Metaneo* occurs frequently in the New Testament, while *metamelomai* is found only a few times (Mt.21:29, 32; 27:3; 2 Cor.7:8; Heb.7:21). Judas' example clearly shows that *metamelomai* is different from *metaneo* in the New Testament.

Judas regretted his betrayal of Jesus (Mt.27:3), but he did not genuinely repent.

Metaneo is a more implicit, inner reorientation of entire life toward God than outward change of direction, relationship, state, or position of a person or a group. *Metaneo* is inward life change involving psychology and emotional feeling. In Acts 3:19 and 26:20 *metaneo* and *epistrepho* were placed side by side: Peter preached, "Repent, then, and turn to God that your sins may be wiped out" (Acts 3:19). Paul witnessed before Agrippa that people should repent and turn to God (Acts 26:20).

Contrasting this is *epistrepho*, which expresses outward change of attitude, behavior and relationship; *metaneo* signifies an inward change, a turning of inner self or attitudes. *Metanoia* is the noun form of *metaneo*, which means a change of heart or repentance (Lk.24:47). Therefore, repentance and confession are integral parts of conversion. Repentance of sin and confession of faith in Christ is the only condition required to be forgiven by God, to whom man is to turn. God forgives and spiritually adopts and regenerates the person (Jn.1:2; 2 Cor.5:17). The essential issue of conversion is a decision of the heart to turn to God, not by a mere change in deeds. McGavran defines it, "Conversion means a participation in a genuine decision for Christ, a sincere turning from the old gods and evil spirits, and determined purpose to live as Christ would have men live" (1980:341).

Conversion is turning or returning to the Lord. Conversion of nominal Christians is that they return to the Lord, whom they already have known. It is restoration of the broken relationship. But these previously non-Christian Koreans were unaware of the Almighty God and later came to know God and turn from the old spirits they had once served.

The Korean Process of Conversion

Conversion was an instant and radical experience or turning to the Lord in the case of the Philippian jailer, the Egyptian eunuch, and the Apostle Paul. But it was not that way for everyone. The cases of Peter and the other apostles were different from Paul's. Conversion seemed to take place gradually for the Peter and the rest of the apostles.

Paul did not impose his own pattern of conversion upon others. He shows agony and yet patience throughout his pastoral letters to the Corinthians, Galatians, and Colossians, which were churches struggling with immorality, immaturity, syncretism, and schisms among new believers.

Tippett viewed conversion as the process of two phases in motion: separation from the old context and incorporation into the new. He developed a schematization of the conversion process into three different periods: 1. Period of Awareness, 2. Period of Decision, and 3. Period of Incorporation. Also, these three different time units were differentiated by two distinct points: point of realization and point of encounter. According to Tippett the point of encounter is the climax of the decision in the process of conversion (1973:123). In Figure 4 I have applied his model to a typical Korean Nazarene process of conversion in on the right.

Figure 4
PROCESS OFCONVERSION

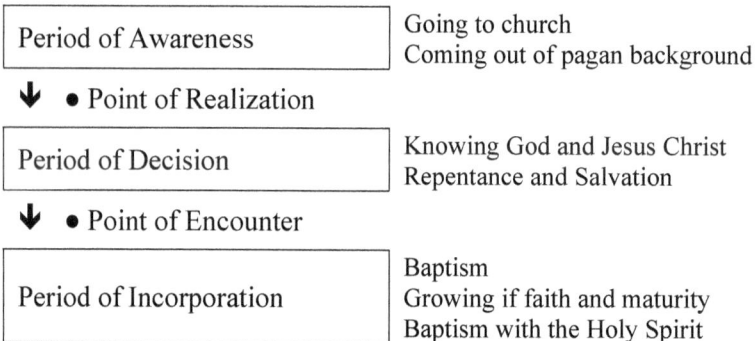

Period of Awareness	Going to church Coming out of pagan background

↓ • Point of Realization

Period of Decision	Knowing God and Jesus Christ Repentance and Salvation

↓ • Point of Encounter

Period of Incorporation	Baptism Growing if faith and maturity Baptism with the Holy Spirit

Coming out of the pagan backgrounds of shamanism, Buddhism and Confucianism, people come to church by decision to depart from the old background. They are new converts who have begun to turn away from the old allegiances, but have not yet completely done so. Upon hearing the message of Jesus Christ, they realize the need of salvation. Then they repent by the conviction of the Holy Spirit during a retreat or evangelistic campaign, dawn prayer meeting, or midnight prayer. Wallace's revitalization process (1956), which deals with general culture change, involves steps similar to the conversion process.[1]

The Korean conversion process is often described by "going to church" ("kyohei e kada") and believing in Christ ("Iesu mitta"). Going to church means that they now believe in God and worship Him instead of demons, ancestral spirits, or fetishes and other objects. It is totally different where nominality is prevalent and going to church may be done as a matter of custom—the form and the meaning between the two are different.

Traditionally in America, even nominal believers might go to church every Sunday. But there is no factor of persecution or difficulty in breaking from ethical and moral norms such as ancestor veneration. Going to church in Korea means that people should abandon the ancestral spirits—the living dead of the family and consanguineous group. For this serious offense, "going to church" can result in ostracism or persecution.

American converts would be considered transformed when forsaking worldly habits such as drinking or smoking, while Koreans are considered transformed when giving up the idolatry of their folk religion, concubinage and ancestral worship.

Entire Sanctification

Koreans have a concept of the sacred and profane, which is rooted in Buddhism and shamanism. Thus it is relatively easy for them to understand a life of holiness. At issue here is the power of God for living a life of holiness. I believe that through the Book of Acts we see that a life of holiness manifests the power of the Holy Spirit rather than outward form and that outward form is a natural result of a radical transformation of inner life. The power of God was on those who lived a holy life.

A shaman heals the sick, exorcises evil spirits and foretells the future. Thus, Koreans are interested in a God who has more power than shamanistic gods. Koreans expect the power of a holy life to be evidenced not only in lifestyle but also as an answer to insecurity, future uncertainty, and demonic oppression. But due to different theological, social and cultural backgrounds, Nazarene theology of conversion and general rules for Christian life are difficult to apply to the Korean church.

To Koreans, holiness could be emphasized as having wholeness in body, soul, and spirit by emphasis on the power of healing and deliverance by the Holy Spirit. This is sanctification. The deep level issues of conversion and sanctification, and what they mean to Koreans, as compared to Americans, is at the very core of doing theology in context.

As believers gather together in community, ecclesiological questions arise. The most significant contextual problem at this point is that of the nature of leadership.

Leadership Issues

Studying leadership structures of Korean society will help us to understand Korean leadership in the church. Koreans largely come from villages with a traditional mentality. Now due to mass migration of rural people into urban areas, the urban population of Seoul has increased to over ten million and continues to increase. Yet while people are living in the modern city, their roots remain in the village. Koreans living in Los Angeles are from both urban and rural areas of Korea, yet their mental map[2] is rooted in the traditional social structure. Urbanization for them is still a recent phenomenon.

Three distinctive elements affect Korean leadership structure. In order to discuss the first element, that of ruler—subject relationship, we must understand social class status. We no longer have a rigid class system, yet status mentality still operates in the Korean community. As I mentioned earlier, during the Yi Dynasty social status was divided into seven ranks: royalty, the *yangba*n (nobility), the *hyangban* and *toban* (second class nobility), the *jung-in* (commoners), the *so-ol* (offspring of concubines), *sangmin* (low cast) and *chunmin* (outcast). These statuses were ascribed, determined by birth, and were far removed from modern urban social structure in which people achieve status.

In contemporary Korean rural society, status systems are made up of three major categories: *yangban, sangmin, and chunmin* (Man Gap Lee 143). The *yangban* (technically offspring of persons with a qualified position in royal government ranging to four generations preceding or following) are grouped with hyangban and *toban* (technically offspring of people with no qualified royal government officials appearing in the families for four generations). *Sangmin* are equated with *jung-in* (commoners who hold farming, commerce, and handicraft occupations). *Chunmin* are butchers, dancers, fortunetellers, and small innkeepers. But as people move to the big cities, fewer distinctions can be found. According to Man Gap Lee, "Today, those of *yangban* and *sangmin* origin do not appear to have any conspicuous conflicts in daily life, even though a covert sense of superiority among the yangban may cause overt conflict on some occasions" (1982:145).

Though people cooperate well and do not discriminate on the surface level, they avoid intermarriage. This gives evidence of the survival of a caste-oriented village mentality among Koreans. Also, it is well known that in Korea there are many villages, such as my own, that are home to a predominant consanguineous group. Man Gap Lee defines a consanguineous group as "the aggregation of the offspring under the same ancestors over four generations, which is larger than a kingroup" (121). This consanguineous group[3] is always blood related and resides in one village together or scattered over different regions. They meet annually for ancestral worship and to take care of gravesites.

Yuji is an informal opinion leader in a village who is seated in the *yangban* class among retired government officials, though occasionally a wealthy *toban* can be a *yuji* too. Of famous celebrities or big names in a community it is said, "Mr. so-and-so is *yuji* in our town." Their opinions are highly regarded in group decisions. The term *yuji* is still used in Los Angeles Korean communities.

It seems obvious that the believers' community, the church, cannot be separated from the worldview of the ruler—subject vertical relationship that is fundamental to Korean human relationships.

One problem is that Korean church people do not fit well with American-style democratic leadership, particularly when there are no ruling elders. In Korean culture the individual does not directly express his opinion; rather a group forms a decision and then takes it to the leader. Therefore, there must be different levels of leadership. Generally, Koreans expect the local church to install people as elders as their age and faith increase. Korean society is a male dominated, age-oriented, patriarchal type with a patrilineal and extended family system.

As Lee portrays it, "The consanguineous group in Korea still plays a powerful political role in maintaining the status quo of pre-modern characteristics in Korean society" (1982:132). It is difficult for a politician or man of power to reject what the consanguineous group recommends or requests. Also if a leader of a consanguineous group suggests or proposes something it will depend on the whole group's decision.

Yuji from the consanguineous *yangban* group or the community almost always hold strong influence in leadership. No matter what outward ecclesiological form a Korean church may adopt, the actual inner working of the church will operate along these lines.

Let us look at the patterns of leadership structure in a village and the influence of *yuji* in supporting the official village chief. This will highlight the distinctive characteristics of Korean village mentality, which conflict with American democratic leadership patterns. Lee categorizes five different types of leadership patterns as illustrated in Figure 5. According to these diagrams of the five leadership patterns, we can gather that the *ri*-chief (local official of basic geographical unit) is supported by the *yuji* (leaders of small villages or group). Individuals always gather around the informal leaders, *yuji*, to form opinions, and the small congregated groups are around the formal leaders.

Type 1 is a leadership structure in which all villagers support an informal leader, and all the informal leaders support the formal leader without serious conflicts. This type consists of *sangmin* and *yangban* without consanguineous ties (except the informal leaders who lead the small groups). This type is more conducive to democratic development because the villagers are independent and equal in class.

Type 2 is formed with only one dominant consanguineous group. The formal leader often comes from the members of this group and is supported by the informal leaders. Individuals who do not belong to the consanguineous group support the informal leader, though without a strong sense of participation. If the group is well integrated, this leadership structure will make group decisions to support the same candidate during an election. The

formal leader or informal leader will influence the group, and
because of the group dynamics the leadership structure will be
strong and stable and will not suffer from inability to promote
village-wide cooperative activity.

Figure 5
FIVE TYPES OF LEADERSHIP PATTERNS
(Adapted from Man Gap Lee 1982:159)

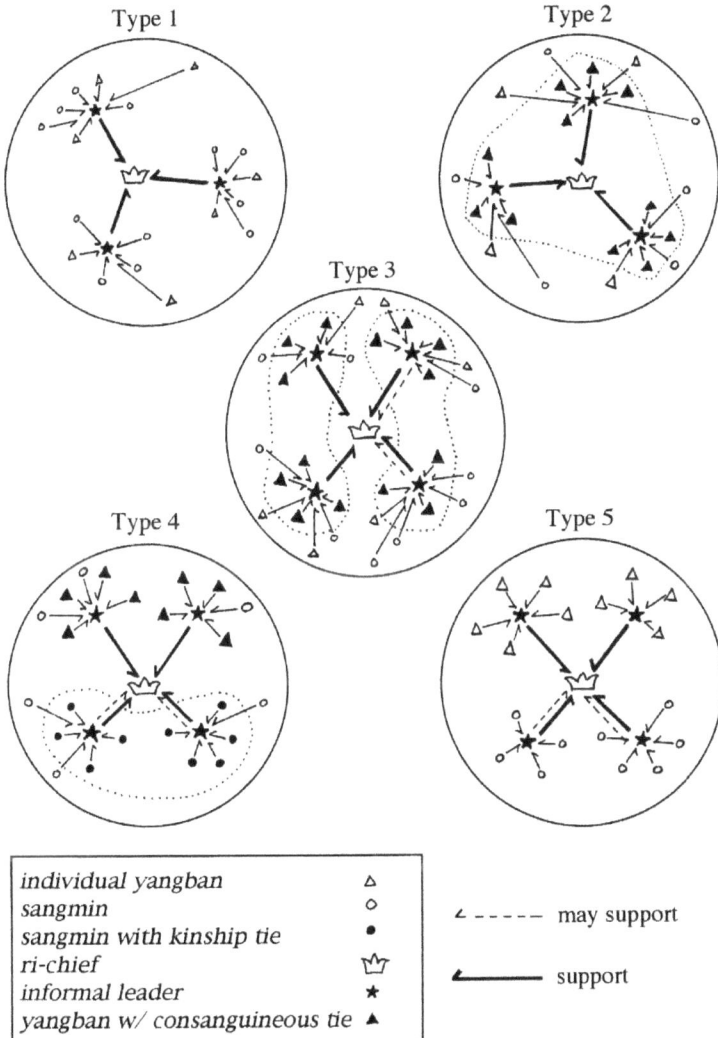

individual yangban	△
sangmin	○
sangmin with kinship tie	●
ri-chief	♕
informal leader	★
yangban w/ consanguineous tie	▲

∠ - - - - - may support

∠———— support

Type 3 is often found in villages where two or three different
competitive consanguineous yangban groups exist. The *ri*-chief

will be chosen from the strongest among the groups. The other group may or may not support him depending on the possible conflicts. At an election each group will vote for its own candidate. This leadership structure has difficulty achieving integration.

Type 4 occurs very seldom but is seen in a case where a consanguineous *yangban* group and a group of *sangmin* have the same family name and place of origin. The latter group has no formal association, though they will be called consanguineous (which reveals a strong division of *yangban* and *sangmin*). If the *ri*-chief comes from the *sangmin*, then he may be supported by the *sangmin* group and consanguineous yangban group when the yangban has a higher official position, such as the town administration deputy. This leadership structure has a high potential for conflict because of the potential for insults from one group to the other.

Type 5 is also rare but is found where two *yangban* and *sangmin* groups exist without any consanguineous ties. These groups are different in status and social background. The individual *yangbans* have no consanguineous basis and no dominant relationship. Thus, the *sangmin* would not recognize the yangban as being superior, while the *yangban* desire to remain as a superior class in order to enjoy their privileges. This relational dynamic easily causes conflicts. An example of this kind of conflict occurred at a village funeral in a *yangban's* family. The *yangban* told some young *sangmin* to carry the coffin (a job only for the lower caste). The *sangmin* refused. As a result a conflict arose between the *yangban* and *sangmin* groups.

The Need of Informal Leaders

Consanguineous kin relationship and traditional status background are still basic factors in the leadership structure of Korean villages, even if the villagers are becoming egalitarian from the push of governmental efforts. The five diagrams clarify how people's decision-making processes are not individualistic but group oriented around an informal leader (*yuji*).

The traditional village leadership reflects the group oriented self of the Koreans. Koreans have difficulty thinking of themselves as individuals and cannot free themselves from vertical relationships within the group. Therefore, decision making is always more group oriented than individual oriented. And a group of any kind is formed by an informal or formal leader who is an opinion leader of the group. Therefore, this worldview affects the leadership structure of Korean immigrant churches in general as follows:

Pastor (senior)
Pastors (associate, assistant, youth, children)
Elders (ordained by local church)
Kwonsa (ordained by local church)
Deacon (ordained by local church)
Deacon (temporary, appointed)
Laity (baptized)

The previous illustration shows the vertical relationship and at the same time the different ranks of leadership. Since the Church of the Nazarene limits a church to having thirteen deacons and ruling elders, it is very difficult for Koreans to adjust because of their traditional leadership mentality.

In addition, Korean churches of any denomination are generally strongly autonomous. They are local-church oriented and, therefore, weak in responding to central government. Members of Korean churches of the Nazarene are required in America to reorient their worldview in order to adjust to a central leadership structure. The language and cultural barriers are other factors aggravating their weakness in coping with central church government.

Korean churches are also centers where the attempt to preserve Korean cultural identity is visible. Korean churches are expected to be at the forefront of preserving Korean language, identity, and values. In other words the church is expected to be the center of resistance to cultural assimilation.

Historically the church was the central post of Korean identity during the Japanese colonial period. Spencer J. Palmer suggests several reasons:

First, of the thirty-three patriots who signed the Declaration of Independence in March 1919, sixteen were Protestant Christians, and the Samil Movement was centered around the schools and the churches of the Protestant denominations. Second, their Bibles have always been printed in Hangul to reach the general population. Third, Protestant churches operate seven universities, fourteen theological schools, forty middle and high schools for boys, and twenty middle and high schools for girls. Fourth, the churches operate a total of six hundred social welfare institutes, conduct anti-vice campaigns and so forth (1966:87–108).

Palmer's reasons have proven true through historical developments in Korea and the important role the Korean church has played for Koreans in America in their expectation of the church to be at the forefront of preserving Korean identity.[4]

Today in the United States, the second generation is educated under an American school system and American teachers. Since they have little opportunity to learn Hangul (the Korean writing system, Korean parents try to preserve their children's identity as Koreans and ask churches to offer various language and cultural programs. Saturday *Hangul hakyo* (Korean language school) is the most effective tool to teach customs and values of Korean culture. Korean Bible memory verse contests and summer trips to Korea are similar activities for children in some churches.

Because the church is the only place where Koreans worship and sing in their own language and culture, and because the church offers counseling, fellowship, mutual aid, and countless minor services, it helps its members cope with American society. Thus, the church becomes the center of preserving Korean culture and naturally prevents full assimilation.

Having generally raised the major areas of cultural, theological and ecclesiological tension, we shall move toward concrete discussion on what contextual changes will make Nazarene churches more incarnationally appropriate for Koreans.

Chapter 8

CONTEXTUALIZATION AND CONCLUSION: TOWARD DOING THEOLOGY FOR KOREAN NAZARENES IN SOUTHERN CALIFORNIA

We now come to the objective of all the previous discussions. We shall conclude by illustrating ways that these observations apply to Korean churches in America. My hope is that suitable changes can be made and new programs and policies introduced that will foster growth among Korean churches.

This closing chapter will review contextual models from which we have gleaned insights. Out of this I will discuss the concept of container and contents and lead toward the development of what I have called a "trajectory principle." Following that I will propose recommendations for contextualizing in cultural, theological, and ecclesiological areas.

A New Perspective

As a conclusion I will present a principle of contextualization, which may help the American Church of the Nazarene in reaching out to Korean immigrants. My hope is to give concrete suggestions for understanding what contextualization demands in this Korean-American situation. It is a working principle that attempts to show

how cultural distance modifies and guides the needed contextualization.

Contributions of the Existing Contextual Models

The contextualization models in Chapter 3 assist us in confronting the Korean-American problems. The Translation Model presupposes that the Christian message is, in essence, supra-cultural. This model helps us find a dual foci, that of content and context, and guides us in how conflicts may be resolved in terms of functional or dynamic equivalence.[1] It is the Translation Model that develops the concept of content and container.

The Semiotic Model contributes insights on how to listen to a culture in terms of its own symbols in order to discover not only the major symbols around which a contextualized theology can be developed, but also the need to watch carefully where change in those symbols is taking place. We learn to observe cultural themes with a magnifying glass through which we can postulate a contextualized, "homegrown" theology.

The other contextualization models that were discussed have also helped in developing what I call the trajectory principle. The value of the Anthropological Model here is that it assumes much in terms of the culture, that truth discovered within the culture is extremely important. Genuine contextualization requires analysis of the deep levels of rituals and language. In the Korean context this model helps to analyze shamanistic rituals and cultural and linguistic behavior in relation to cultural themes.

The strength of the Praxis Model for the problems raised by recent immigrants and their families is that there must be constant reflection on history and appropriate action in which people themselves effect change. It is necessary to learn to reflect on the past for evaluation of a theology and to apply the outcome of that process for doing theology in a new context.

The Synthetic Model shows that contextualization needs to be in a dialectical and dialogical process. This is because every culture needs to share its uniqueness in the discovery of what is true and valid with others. It calls for open-endedness, which is sometimes difficult for those who teach the standard of instantaneous holiness.

Contents and Containers

In leading up to a discussion of the trajectory principle, let us look at contextualization as having two components. We speak of contents and containers (or wine and wineskin). These two components are so intimately related that one invariable affects the other. Thus we must deal with both. The metaphor of "contents" suggests Nazarene doctrine, particularly of conversion, and the holiness emphasis. The container is the ecclesiological structure of the Nazarene Church, particularly the leadership structure.

Let's go back to our Los Angeles grocery store, with which we began, where the clientele was predominantly Korean, the commodities sold were oriented toward these new people. As the products on the shelves changed, so did the labels on the jars, bags, and boxes. To attempt to package the new Korean foods in the previously used jars, bags, and boxes would have produced chaos, frustration, and unsold goods.

The principle is that when a previous message must address the needs and questions of a new receptor, new facets or emphases of that message must be recognized that have not been recognized before (such as the issues raised by Korean-American Nazarenes). Likewise, the container (church structure) must also be made appropriate to the new receptor.

To lead into my proposed principle, suppose these containers with their contents were propelled through space to destinations of varying distances. Aside from modern self-propelled rocketry, I believe traditional aeronautical principles would require that the progressively distant destinations would require different densities of propellants (contents) in the rocket housing, the containers.

I suggest that reaching the distant destinations might also require a differently designed "container" than the one suitable for reaching the nearer destination. An important point to remember is that neither the "contents" nor "container" of one rocket would in any way nullify or contradict those of another. Their differences are calculated only for the purpose of reaching their respective targets. In addition, these different rockets would have to be aimed on trajectories of varying heights to reach their respective destinations.

The Trajectory Principle

If I were to attempt to fire a rocket from Kansas City to Dallas, I would have to find the proper trajectory and path if the rocket is to hit the target—not too high and not too low, the comparatively short distance would call for a comparatively low trajectory.

If I attempted to fire the same rocket to Mexico City, I would have to open up the angle for a higher trajectory in order to cover the greater distance. If I attempted to fire the same rocket to Seoul, I would have to further adjust the angle to gain a still higher trajectory in order for the rocket to hit the remote target. I would also have to be very sure that the fuel is of adequate volume and density.

In the same way cultures are distant in varying degrees. In church growth terms, "E-1," "E-2" and "E-3" are used to designate cultural distance with regard to evangelism.[2] "E" refers to "evangelism" and 1, 2, 3 refer to barriers between the transmitter and receiver of the gospel message. "E-1" would be culturally much the same as the primary culture and require little, if any, contextualization (as from Kansas City to Dallas). The barrier here is that between the church and the world. "E-2" adds to the church barrier the barrier of reaching a people who are culturally and linguistically distinct, yet somewhat similar (as the difference between Anglo-American and Mexican cultures).

"E-3" adds to these the additional, or greater, barrier of a distant culture and language, one that is totally different from one's own (as the difference between Anglo-American and Korean). Note that the terms "E-1," "E-2," and "E-3" in themselves are not designations of geographical distance but of cultural distance.

These three barriers, or degrees of difference between cultures are relative to the departure point. In the trajectory model of Figure 6, the degree of contextualization necessary for the message to be on target may suggest the degree of angle at which the rocket must be fired to gain the trajectory necessary to hit the target. Biblical truth is applicable to each context, but may be expressed differently.

The trajectory itself represents the contextualization process. It is, first of all, culturally relevant to its starting point. In this case we have in mind the standards of the general Church of the Nazarene in the U.S.A. The rocket in its flight is obviously not static. It is in constant forward motion. The motion itself may be compared to the process of contextualization itself—always in motion. The more culturally distant the target group, the higher from the horizon and longer the trajectory, or degree of contextualization, must be.

This is the model's fundamental portrayal of contextualization theory: the more distant the target, the higher a trajectory is required. That is, the greater the cultural distance, the greater the degree of contextualization required. And for the process the appropriate "contents" and "container" must be designed.

A longer trajectory to a more distant target also requires more thrust. Likewise, contextualizing for a culturally distant group will require more energy and investment than for a culturally near group.

Figure 6
THE TRAJECTORY PRINCIPLE

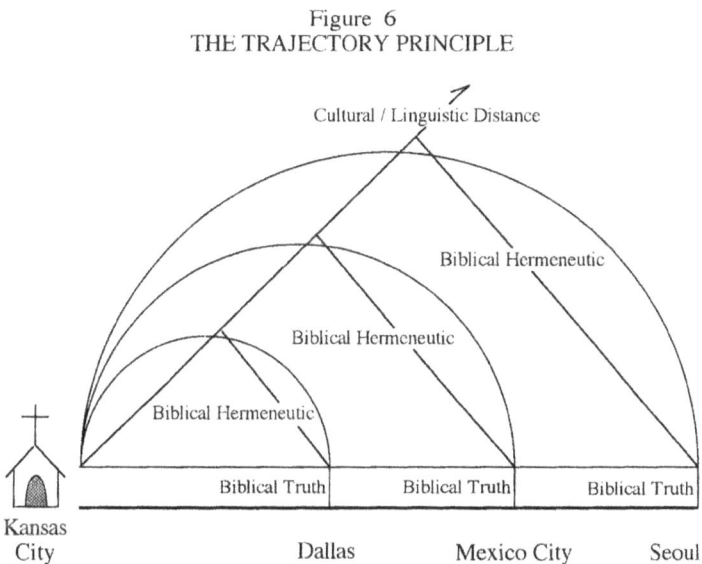

The trajectory principle takes three things quite seriously: 1) biblical hermeneutics, involving God's revelation: the contents; 2) communication, dealing with translation and interpretation: the container; 3) cultural hermeneutics, dealing with cultural forms and meanings of the contents and containers: the trajectory. The apex of this principle is where biblical hermeneutics parallel cultural hermeneutics.

If the rocket itself is the container of the message (Nazarene church structure)—and the contents of the rocket is Nazarene doctrine (e.g. conversion and holiness doctrine), then we may observe how, using the trajectory principle, these must both be re-expressed (contextualized) in varying degrees to reach culturally distant target groups. If the group is not being adequately reached, as I have argued, then both the contents and form of the delivery systems, the "rockets," should be critiqued and modified.

First-generation Korean immigrants are encountering difficulties with the leadership structure of the Church of the Nazarene in America due to their linguistic and cultural distance. But even though second-generation Koreans are born and raised in America, they may face many of the same cultural problems that their parents faced because they have been raised in Korean homes. It is necessary for the Koreans to work with the Americans in establishing biblical principles of contextualization to meet the demands of these cultural differences with traditional American Nazarenes.

Following are thoughts for contextualization in problem areas I originally raised and dealt with in the preceding chapter.

Contextualizing Cultural Issues

Related to the four cultural themes discussed in Chapter 6, I will briefly review the essential differences and suggest some paths toward contextualization.

Sacred and Profane: Time and Space

At this point let us apply the cultural themes we observed in Chapter 5. The ideas of sacred and profane among Koreans are embodied in elements of time and space and are expressed especially through rituals, which are not part of North American secular life. In the American mind the natural and supernatural are kept as separate entities with relatively little attention given to clean and unclean concepts in the governance of daily life.

The biblical doctrine of holiness has two important elements: separation and cleansing. These are separation to God from the world and cleansing from all that is unclean. This is easily comprehended by the Korean mind because of their pre-existing concept of sacredness, as we have already discussed. It is a matter of changing allegiance from their gods to God, of being separated from the world unto God, of God's presence manifest more in power than in form.

The Korean approach to the holiness concept is manifest by a fervent prayer life, including dawn prayer, midnight prayer, and all-night prayer in the church sanctuary. This is because Koreans believe the power of the Holy Spirit comes through prayer but also that is especially important to pray in the "sacred space" of the church. But since American churches do not perceive prayer in these ways, when they see Korean Christians insisting on praying in the sanctuary, they might naturally respond, "Go home and pray in your closet. God is everywhere." In one case it was requested that they pay overnight boarding expense since they slept in the sanctuary!

These misunderstandings occur because the American expression of holiness is different from the Korean expression. The American understanding of holiness insists that with the help of the Holy Spirit, one abstains from all intoxicating drink, smoking, sexual immorality, and immodesty in dress and makeup for women.

Both Korean men and women have the same positive respect for that standard, and in addition express a life of holiness through an active prayer life, including midnight and dawn prayer meetings. But the most important and difficult problem is how to stop both divination and ancestral worship. Korean culture does not prohibit women's adornment but definitely expects modesty and virtue of both men and women.

These values of virtue and modesty are taught in moral education, which starts from kindergarten in the Korean educational system. At the beginning and end of every school day all Korean students receive moral or ethical education. But at the same time Korean culture endorses ancestral worship, divination of all kinds, concubinage, and even gambling. Therefore, the Korean Church of the Nazarene must stress a holiness lifestyle, which addresses the problems typical of Korean culture.

In the American Nazarene churches the entire sanctification experience is a crisis event that takes place, it seems, at an open altar or prayer during a camp meeting. Through this experience believers are separated by God from religious nominalism and the secular, carnal world. Koreans tend, on the other hand to seek and pursue the Lord by fasting and praying at mountain prayer centers or dawn or midnight prayer meetings. When they experience sanctification, they are convicted regarding the old Korean lifestyle, friends, and habits. For them holiness is more a separation from traditional beliefs, religious practices, customs, and ancestral spirits, rather than from nominalism or worldliness.

Causality: *Palcha* and Cause and Effect

Causality for Koreans traditionally lies in fate, or *palcha*, while for Americans it lies more prominently in scientific cause and effect. As Jean Piaget proposes, childhood development influences adult behavioral patterns and psychology: "It is much the same when we say, in accordance with ordinary common sense, that ducks have webbed feet so as to swim better" (Piaget 1969:259). This statement agrees with the American search for empirical causes and effect.

In the Korean church the concept of fate or destiny is theologically reformulated as foreknowledge and predestination in Christ (e.g., Ro.8:29; Eph.1:5).[3] This is core causality concept that must be dealt with. *Palcha* must be replaced with election if the people are to make a proper transition into a Christian way of thinking without syncretizing *palcha* underneath a theology of free will. Thus, when developing a Bible study series, freedom needs to be given to those seeking to transform the Korean mind and heart form the idea of *palcha* toward a biblical understanding of the sovereignty and providence of God.

Self and Other: Corporativeness and Individualism

Self and other in the Korean context is understood in terms of being a corporate person, being part of a group. This easily lends itself to accommodating the biblical doctrine of the Church's being one body in Christ, the household of God. The Korean understanding of group self is to some degree analogous to the Church as the body of Christ. Decisions are made by groups, such as the family, clan, village, school, company, organization, and nation. A local church may easily be included among these categories as Koreans seek ways to maintain the extended family system.

Marriage is a familial decision rather than an individual's own decision. Divorce is, therefore, looked upon as being failure that brings shame upon the collective family and thus should not be made known. Nouns of address like grandparent, uncle, aunt, brother, or sister, are used even when there is no blood relationship. Group-self demands obedience and sacrifice of the individual self, which is contrary to the American individualistic self.

Children go to their father's church to fulfill their obligation of filial piety and to please their parents. If a father or grandfather becomes an elder of a church, all the family must attend that church because of the support expected for the person holding the office of elder. Naturally, the corporativeness of self affects evangelism and reinforces the potential for people movements. This extended family system also influences the church government system in a variety of ways, making it almost clannish at times.

The American self centers on self-reliance and is fundamentally independent of society, family, and others. Naturally, the American self does not incline toward an extended family; rather, it centers on the nuclear family. The American self pursues freedom, rights, success, happiness, and security for the individual rather than for the group. Thus, American parents have no problem in allowing their grown children to go to other churches.

The group-self mentality contributes to both rapid church growth as well as sudden splits in Korean churches. Ignoring this group-self dimension when structuring the leadership of a church will invariably create a foreign atmosphere among Koreans, and ultimately hinder growth. I will discuss this subject further in terms of church government and leadership.

Relationships: Horizontal Egalitarianism and Vertical Ruler-Subject

Korean relationships are essentially vertical, as in the manner of ruler-subject, being rooted in Confucian ideology. I have discussed Confucianism's five cardinal principles, which have generated the vertical ruler-subject relationship and created a title-oriented society. Thus, a Korean is called Mr., Miss, or Mrs. only when they do not have any other business, social, official, or religious titles. Titles themselves maintain the vertical relationship between two or more people.

This Korean worldview deeply affects the leadership, structure, and patterns of Korean churches. For example, a problem arises when a district licensed minister pastors a church but people do not address him or her as a "pastor." They cannot call him or her "pastor" because that person may be licensed but not ordained. The Korean language does not distinguish between pastor, minister, or reverend; all are called *moksa*.

In Korean culture the term for pastor, *moksa*, refers only to an ordained minister, and the ordained minister is higher than a licensed minister in leadership structure.[4] Therefore, people will insist on calling that person *cheondosa*, which means "evangelist." In the American mindset this is not a great problem; but Koreans have a very difficult time pastoring under a district license, because the church people simply will not respect them as pastors unless they've first been ordained. I am not suggesting that any changes ought to be made but simply describing the culturally related problems of Koreans.

In English "you" is the second person pronoun for everyone, whether old or young, or of high or low social status. Korean on the other hand requires the use of a complicated system of honorifics whenever referring to another person. American individuals have rights and power in voting, and church is operated by votes and committees. Koreans on the other hand are very weak in the democratic process and fear that it will cause leadership to suffer a lack of authority.

When a Korean merges into the American system, he or she may have difficulties. For example a Korean pastor wanted to use a classroom in a multi-congregational church, but a custodian who was cleaning there said, "No." He said this because the pastor did not have permission from the property committee of the church. The Korean pastor was shocked, but in a busy American church it is natural, even necessary.

Nazarene regulations covering the number of church board members and trustees seem to be related to this egalitarianism and are appropriate for the American context. But in the Korean Church a few adjustments would increase the effective operation of a church. Trustees might be seen as ruling elders to empower laypersons to serve the body of Christ. This in turn could connect with the Korean need for lay leaders to have titles as elders or deacons to lead and care for the believers. Accordingly, it is initially easy to apply biblical principles of vertical relationships through which lay people may serve the body of Christ in building up the lay people.

Therefore, I recommend that many small group leaders be installed who can direct, counsel, teach, and pray with the members in order to replace the blood ties and the other natural social units.

Contextualizing Theological Issues

Since the Nazarenes are downstream of Methodism, which emphasizes the doctrine of entire sanctification, it is appropriate for us to look at biblical holiness in Wesleyan tradition prior to approaching doctrinal issues.

Biblical Holiness in Wesleyan Tradition

The words "holiness" *qodesh* and "holy" *qadosh*, with their cognates, occur 605 times in the Old Testament. These references are very often used in relation to cults and rituals (Purkeiser, et al. 1977:164), yet it is holiness that describes the primary attribute of God. Beyond this, the holiness of God is a dominant and unifying theme of the Bible. God commanded the Israelites through Moses, "Consecrate yourselves and be holy" (Lev.20:7). By this he meant, "set yourselves apart" to God in a truly radical way.

Holiness is also communicated through God's power, which comes upon inanimate objects such as Mt. Sinai, the ark of God, and the place of the temple (Ex.19:12–13; 2 Sam.6:6–10; 2 Chr.7:1–3). Gerhard Von Rad clarified God's holiness primarily as being separation in terms of relationship to God. He pointed out: "If an object or a place, or a day or a man is sanctified, this means to begin with only that it is separated, assigned to God, for God is the source of all that is holy…. It has been rightly observed that the term indicates relationship more than a quality" (1962:205).

Separation indicates consecration to God for a new relationship rather than consecration for quality of life only. In the Greek New Testament God's holiness is translated by the word *hagios* (holy). *Hagios* means "holy" or "sanctified," or "make holy" (sanctify). Holiness in the Old and New Testament addressed the majestic glory, righteousness and power of the very nature of God.

Jesus prayed for sanctification of the believers by the truth (Jn.17:17) and the apostle Paul prayed that the Thessalonians be sanctified through and through by the work of the Holy Spirit (1 Th.5:23). Such sanctification is ultimately expressed as love.

Love was first on Wesley's heart when he spoke of holiness. Separation to God and love for God is the basis of holiness. Wesley emphasizes entire sanctification as being "neither more nor less than pure love—love expelling sin and governing both heart and life" (Peters 1956:58–59; Williams 1960:183).

Wesley affirmed the importance of faith as the only condition for sanctification, that sanctification was by faith and faith alone. Holiness becomes manifest in terms of an unbroken relationship with Christ, the Holy One. In one of his sermons Wesley spoke of "Holiness as the Circumcision of the Heart," which he described as that "habitual disposition of the soul which, in the sacred writings, is termed holiness; and which directly implies, the being cleansed from sin" (quoted in Williams 175).

In his book *A Plain Account of Christian Perfection* Wesley dealt at length with what he meant by "perfection." In speaking of the "sanctified" he said, "They are not perfect in knowledge. They are not free from ignorance, no, nor from mistake. We are no more to expect any living man to be infallible, than to be omniscient. They are not free from infirmities" (Works XI:374).

Humans can never be perfect in the sense that they can be independent from Christ. Wesley meant a perfection that is free from known sin, yet in need of forgiveness.

Because of his or her unbroken relationship with Christ, the "perfect Christian" becomes more and more aware of his or her moral, psychological, and intellectual imperfections and weaknesses. Thus, entire sanctification is not a final experience, but is a process that has a beginning point and leads a Christian to seek Christ aggressively and to grow in grace more and more.

Sanctification is entering into a new and intimate relationship with Christ, reaching the point of complete dependence on him. By holiness teaching it is essentially meant that the qualities of God become the aim and object of living the Christian life.

Holiness as Separation from Old Korean Customs and Traditions.

The description of entire sanctification in the 1989 *Manual* is almost identical to that of the 1911 *Manual*, which was written in the formative stages of the Nazarene Church. It is imperative, therefore, that Koreans be entirely sanctified through the baptism with the Holy Spirit. Presently, Korean unbelievers are bound by the fear of demonic powers and elementary spirits.

Entire sanctification will provide them not only with heart cleansing but also with power to cast out demons and to heal the sick, which will better enable them to live apart from the old customs and practices. Because Koreans have been under these powers for several thousand years, and must be separated, the miracle working power of the Spirit becomes a vitally important aspect of a life of holiness.

One thing that may be noted here is that healing played an important part in Nazarene tradition, and the *Manual* states, "Divine Healing is affirmed and believers are urged to pray for the sick." But there seem to be few churches practicing regular healing services. Since God brings wholeness to persons suffering from physical sickness, as well as stress, emotional problems, brokenness, bitterness, and broken relationships, both Americans and Koreans would do well to place greater emphasis on God's healing as a part of regular worship services and special meetings.

General Rules and Cultural Appropriateness

The General rules are clearly laid out in each edition of the *Manual*; these are the do's and don'ts for the Nazarenes. In the pursuit of holiness the discussion at this point is focused on how to apply these rules to Korean immigrants who have totally different cultural roots.

The original rules for general Christian life in 1989 were dealt with both negatively and positively, and essentially confront evil as understood in the North American context. They are almost identical to those laid down in 1932 and include:

1) Do what is good in the Word of God by faith and practice, including loving God and neighbor as oneself.
2) Avoid evil of every kind, including the profaning of the day of the Lord, either by unnecessary ordinary labor or business, or by holiday diversions.
3) The use of intoxicating liquors as a beverage is forbidden or the trafficking of the same therein, or giving influence to, or voting for the licensing of places for the sale of the same.
4) Quarreling, returning evil for evil, gossiping, slandering, spreading surmises injurious to the good of the name of others.
5) Dishonesty, taking advantage in buying and selling, bearing false witness, and the like fruits of darkness.
6) The indulgence of pride in dress or living, the laying up of treasures on earth; women's modesty in adornment and apparel.
7) Songs, literature, and amusements that are not to the glory of God. The avoidance of such things as lotteries and games of chance, looseness and impropriety of conduct. The avoidance of such places as the theater, the ballroom, the circus and like places. (*Manual* 1932:34, Cf. 1989:39–41).

These rules are no doubt relevant to both American and Korean believers, but additional contextualization seems to be needed for Koreans. Since rules are essential to maintain standards in the holiness tradition, the Korean context would necessitate rules, which are not necessary in the North American context.

Some of the general rules are equally endorsed in Korean culture, which some of the prohibitions touch upon practices that are not commonly done and are already condemned in Korean tradition. Matters not relevant to American culture are naturally given little attention in the *Manual*; in the same way, if Koreans were to write a *Manual*, some matters would be highly emphasized and others would be less emphasized—but what is emphasized would be quite different. In addition to what is emphasized in the *Manual*, the Korean church needs clear directives on at least several issues. Suggestions are as follows.

A Functional Substitute for Ancestral Veneration

The church must prohibit the practices of ancestral veneration and redirect the focus onto living ancestors, i.e., the elderly. Ceasing ancestral veneration is perhaps the primary sign of genuine conversion. But since ancestral veneration is deeply rooted in filial piety, a simple prohibition can never resolve the problem. Such would only result in the practices going underground.

The Korean Nazarene Church could instead propose a functional substitute in the form of a commemoration service in an appropriate place and time which would provide a way for the whole family, especially the children, to express honor and cultivate respect for the family, both living and dead.

A Recognition of Filial Piety Towards Living Parents

While ancestral veneration is the apex of fulfillment of filial duty, the church should teach members to love and care for living parents rather than giving all attention to them after death. I recommend that the church teach Jesus' obedience to God the Father in line with filial piety as the example (Phil.2:5–11). The elderly especially suffer social dislocation because of the transition of cultures and language both at home and in the community.

In answer to this, I recommend the creation of a multi-purpose room or center in Korean Churches of the Nazarene as a place for the elderly to gather to rest, fellowship, and if possible, learn how to adjust to the new culture. For example, the church could provide opportunities for prayer meetings, language and culture learning, and structured fellowship session sin order to maximize the meaning of their lives rather than becoming a burden to their offspring. This is in line with the blessings promised by God when we keep His commandment to honor our parents (Ex.20:12).

Prohibition of Divination and Idolatrous Practices

Drugs, dancing or dressing immodestly are not as high agenda problems for Koreans as they are for Americans, since Korean culture is more conservative and traditional and people generally refrain from these acts anyway. However, in addition to ancestral veneration, the majority of non-Christian Koreans are deeply immersed in practices related to divination of all kinds, demonism, polygamous ideas, and animistic practices.

Therefore, if there are to be rules toward holiness, they must prohibit palm reading, face reading, *saju* (divination by the year, month, date, and hour of birth), consulting with shaman and fortunetellers and all involvement in any idolatrous acts that they follow. These kinds of practices can be corrected by teaching the Scripture and experiencing the power of the Holy Spirit. Nurturing and growing new Christians in the knowledge of God with sensitivity to these cultural habits is exceedingly important if they are to be led into a Christian way.

I recommend that the general church give freedom to the Korean Church in these various areas and benefit them by officially recognizing standards relevant to the Korean context insofar as they are harmonious with the Bible and Nazarene ethos.

Conversion

With such a divergence of cultural assumptions, value systems and ways of expression, the process of conversion itself can differ from culture to culture. While Koreans in America can become Christians (and Nazarene), we have seen that it is difficult for them to become just like American Nazarenes. Likewise, their process of conversion will not be the same as that of Americans.

The Nazarene *Manual* does not use the term conversion but articulates the theological process of conversion as "justification, regeneration and adoption [which] are simultaneous in the experience of seekers after God and are obtained upon the condition of faith, preceded by repentance; and that to this work and state of grace the Holy Spirit bears witness" (*Manual* 1989:33).

As we have looked at Korean worldview, which is deeply associated with polydemonic elements, the process of conversion requires a hermeneutic that is somewhat different form that of American culture. A common point of departure leading to conversion is when a Korean decides to go to church before receiving Jesus Christ. When a father goes to church, the whole family usually goes with him. Turning from old traditions and customs is the way most Koreans begin their conversion. It is a gradual process: After attending church and hearing the gospel, they eventually make a decision and later receive the baptism with the Holy Spirit and live a life of holiness.

In relations to group orientation in conversion, McGavran writes:

> Conversion means participation in a genuine decision for Christ, a sincere turning from the old gods and evil spirits, and determined purpose to live as Christ would have men live. The individual decisions within a people movement exhibit all these marks. It is a series of multi-individual, mutually interdependent conversions (1980:341).

For Koreans in a group-oriented society, this means that it is a group decision rather than an individual breaking away from the community. The group (family) makes a decision to attend a church and to believe, leaving the old gods and spirits, but perhaps not everyone genuinely repents. They may belong to church, not necessarily to the Kingdom of God. Yet they are on the way to conversion.

The conversion process is complete when each person as an individual sincerely repents of sin and receives forgiveness from God. Many of the churchgoers, although not yet fully converted, are careful to follow leads from other members of the group.

In 1989, I personally led thirty people to Christ, including Korean college students and adults who had been attending church but were not yet Christian. Most of them attended church because of a friends' invitation or to preserve harmony in the family. In every case they turned away from the old gods or practices in order to join the church.

The *Manual* of 1911 describes repentance as "a sincere and thorough change of the mind in regard to sin involving a sense of personal guilt and a voluntary turning from sin." Conversion is explained as a change of heart from sin and guilt to forgiveness through repentance. According to the Manual conversion is viewed as a specific point in time. But as we have discussed earlier, conversion can, at least among Koreans, be experienced as a process. Viewing conversion as a process, a new convert must be allowed to go through successive periods or levels of growth.

Contextualizing Ecclesiological Issues

The last area of contextualizing I would like to look at involves Korean participation in church government and the raising up and organizing of pastoral and lay leaders.

Government

Merging of the American eastern, western, and southern holiness movements, brought the necessity of a superintendency. Jurisdictional authority and a system for supervising and assisting local churches was agreed upon. The Church of the Nazarene adopted a representative form of government in which each church elects delegates to various assemblies, manages its own finances, and has charge of all other matters pertaining to local church life. This governmental arrangement has given the denomination a dual congregational/episcopal structure.

In addition, there are two different assemblies, the General and District Assemblies. The General Assembly is the quadrennial meeting of the entire general church. The General Assembly is composed of ministerial and lay delegates in equal numbers, elected by the District Assemblies, and is the supreme legislative body formulating authority for the Church of the Nazarene.

The General Superintendents are elected by a vote of the elders in the General Assembly. A General Superintendent ordains elders, organizes local churches, and presides over the annual District Assemblies. The six General Superintendents are responsible for presiding over District Assemblies on six continents, overseeing world mission work and business of the General Board. All are Anglo-Americans.

The District Assembly is an annual gathering of ordained elders, licensed ministers and lay delegates from local churches. The District Assembly votes for its District Superintendent and chooses an "Advisory Board." There are also boards of Ministerial Studies, Church Properties, Ministerial Benevolence, Evangelism, Christian Life, Home Mission, Ways and Means, District Court Appeals, Sunday School, World Mission Society, and Nazarene Youth International. It should be noted that Koreans rarely attend these assemblies, because they simply do not understand English well enough to participate, and they also feel socially alienated.

The District Superintendent supervises the local churches within his assembly district. All official acts of the District Superintendent are subject to review and revision by the District Assembly. In the local church a pastor must be an ordained elder or licensed minister. An elder or licensed minister may be called to pastor a church after being approved by the District Superintendent and receiving a two-thirds favorable vote by ballot.

The Calling of a Pastor

These procedures cause some contextual problems in the local Korean Church of the Nazarene in the United States. A major one involves the calling of a pastor. It is extremely difficult to call a Korean Nazarene pastor in the United States, since there is only a small number of ordained ministers, and there is a great shortage of associate pastors and pastors of youth and children. This problem points out the urgent need for leadership training for first-generation Korean ministerial candidates.

The Pastoral Review

The other aspect is the regular pastoral review. It is very common that when a Korean pastor plants a church, he stays at that church all his life. The pastor identifies himself with the church and considers the church his God-given, lifelong commitment, which engenders a deep relationship between the pastor and the people. Furthermore, the pastor is superior in the vertical relationship and a spiritual leader to follow and obey. All this makes people feel great difficulty to vote for or against a pastor.

This problem arises from different concepts and styles of pastoral leadership between Americans and Koreans. The Korean parsonage door is always open, and people can visit and eat at the parsonage any time during the week, making the relationship between pastor and sheep tight and strong. Thus it is difficult for them to conduct the pastoral review.

District Cooperation

Koreans often feel alienated from district administration. This does not mean that the district leadership does not love Koreans or care for them. They do. Rather, language and cultural barriers make communication difficult. The District Assembly, camp meetings, and other events are not reaching the Korean heart, because language and cultural differences result in forms meaningful to Americans but not to Koreans.

The publications put out by general headquarters tend not to be applicable to Korean churches. Since Korean Christians cannot appreciate the district or general church benefits, naturally they have little inclination to pay district budgets or general budgets. District Superintendents naturally have difficulty in understanding or dealing with ethnic minority groups, especially those who are culturally distant, such as Koreans. This problem is pronounced in places like Southern California, where the population is heavily multi-ethnic. Therefore, it is important to explore the needs for contextualization in these structural areas.

Pastoral and Lay Leadership

In church leadership patterns we see that as concepts of the pastor are different according to culture, so are concepts of lay leadership. Elders, stewards, their numbers, and training leaders are areas where contextualization would greatly benefit the Korean Church of the Nazarene in America.

We have said that once a Korean pastor is chosen, it is very difficult for a Korean congregation to vote whether the pastor should move or stay. There are other problems as well. The concept and style of pastoral leadership is also different between Americans and Koreans. Korean pastors are esteemed by having spiritual power rather than by being nice people. And when a Korean pastor retires, he will often remain as pastor emeritus. Thus, this expectation of the people creates a different pastoral leadership style, namely, more authoritarian than democratic.

Contextual problems are not only present in calling a pastor but also evident when electing numbers of stewards and the board of trustees in a local church. The *Manual* prescribes that the trustees of the church "shall be no fewer than three nor more than nine in number" (1989:83). I would like to look at this more closely through some related areas.

The Elder System. Because of a hierarchical village mentality, Koreans have many small group leaders in the church of the *yuji* (informal leader) type or of elderly men (*eorun*). An *euron* is a wise elderly man who exercises informal familial and social leadership. It is a widely used term and can be translated as "elder." The biblical term for elder is *changno*, which is used in Korean churches with similar connotations as *euron*.

The Christian "elder" (*changno*) functions like an *eorun* in the church. The term "trustees" is a very awkward word to Korean ears, because in their sacred/profane distinctions, they have difficulty using titles, which are used in secular business. The word *changno* would be a good replacement, because the term is culturally meaningful. Thus far the Korean *Manual* has been using the word "elder" (*changno*) instead of "trustee." These are lay leaders chosen by the congregation and are installed with the laying on of hands by local pastors who are ordained by the Church of the Nazarene. Without doing so, the church in Korea would have great difficulty in growing. Being under the jurisdiction of American districts and the *Manual*, Korean immigrants have great difficulty operating the way churches in Korean do. Thus, this institutional factor is a hindrance to their growth.

The Kwonsa System. The Nazarene office of the steward is one point in which the church's ecclesiology fits well with Koreans. Every Korean church has numerous stewards (*chipsa*). In Korean church structures elders are always men, except in the Methodist Church. For women who then go beyond the level of steward, there exists a position between steward (which can be man or woman) and elder: the *kwonsa*.

The installment of *kwonsa* is also necessary in order to look after women believers and women's issues in the church. Because women outnumber men in most churches, we must consider women for lay leadership so they can encourage, exhort, and correct the younger women (Tit.2:3). Korean culture similarly expects faithful older women to encourage younger women in their faith and to devote themselves to pray for the church. Therefore, it is necessary for the church to give them authority to perform certain assigned ministries. I recently attended an installation service of elders and the consecration of deaconesses (*kwonsa*) in a Korean Church.

This visible recognition is needed for effective lay leadership. In secular Korean culture respect is based on prestige and social standing, but in the body of Christ it is based on faith, love, and ministry gifts. I propose that the *kwonsa* system described in the Korean *Manual* become permissible for Korean Churches of the Nazarene in Southern California.

The Limitation of the Number of Stewards. The *Manual* states that "The stewards of the church shall be no fewer than 3 nor more than 13 in number" (*Manual* 1989:82). This limitation to thirteen may be suitable in the American Church regardless of the size of the church, but a Korean local church may need to have more than thirteen because of the demands on lay leaders within Korean culture. Most Korean churches have as many as twenty stewards if there are more than 100 people in the congregation.

Since Koreans came from a bureaucratic social structure with strong vertical relationships, people are used most effectively when as many qualified people as possible are made stewards. I asked four pastors about this. One who has one 140 people in his congregation has about thirty stewards. Another has seven stewards among a thirty-member congregation. The third has twelve active stewards among his twenty-seven-member congregation. The fourth has five members who are stewards. They also have *kwonsas*, though they did not install them because they came and joined from other denominational churches.

As we have already discussed group self, the order of vertical relationships in the Korean community requires many informal group leaders. Koreans tend to gather together due to their corporate mentality. Therefore, it is absolutely necessary to provide for Koreans to appoint, without limitation, leaders who function as stewards who can direct and care for the newer Christians.

The Shortage of Pastors and the Need for Theological Education by Extension. As I reviewed a brief history of Korean Church of the Nazarene, several pastors tried to pioneer Korean

Nazarene churches. Among them only 40 percent were Nazarene ministers. Most of them were from other denominations. The Korean Church needs Nazarene ministers who received education from Nazarene educational institutions.

The Nazarene Bible College in Colorado Springs, CO, presently offers Theological Education by Extension through the Biblical Teologica in Spanish and the Armenian Bible college, as well as being partner with the Bresee Urban Ministry Training Institute.

These are excellent training opportunities, but first-generation Koreans do not have sufficient English ability to receive a theological education in English. Yet there is an urgent need for formal leadership training of Korean pastors, associate pastors and youth pastors. Would-be Korean Nazarene ministers presently are studying in other denominational Bible colleges. This adversely affects the growth of the Korean Church of the Nazarene in the U.S.A.

This problem must be addressed by the Korean pastors, without expecting the district to take initiation. I suggest that Theological Education by Extension be introduced as a beginning. This could be done through the cooperation of the Church in Korea and perhaps Nazarene Bible College.

Possibly one way to solve this problem in the short range is to invite the workers from the Nazarene Bible College in Korea. But in the longer range this need has to be met within our own structures.

Continuing Education for Existing Pastors. Leadership training should also include the continuing education of existing pastors. They need to receive updated theological and missiological education. Short-term biblical training through workshops and seminars should also be extended to lay leaders. Elders and other lay leaders need to be carefully trained to oversee and care for church members. As the existing pastors are trained, they can in turn train the younger leadership, as well as attend to their own continued renewal.

Dialogue. Each local Korean church also needs to have a coordinator to connect with the district. On the district level American pastors need to gather together with Korean pastors using their facilities. This will open up a form for sharing and for mutual understanding and improvement of relationships.

The Local Church

In addition to leadership, concepts related to the functioning of the local church are culturally related. How to think of new members, Sunday school, worship, budget, use of facilities, and church life are also potential areas for contextualization that could greatly benefit the Korean Church of the Nazarene in America.

Probationary Members. The Nazarene Church allows for probationary members who have all the privileges of full church members, with the exception of voting and holding church office. In Korean culture the idea of probationary members has only negative connotations and carries shame, because it means the person is disqualified to be an insider, leaving that person feeling like an outcast. It is also difficult to translate what the word "probationary" means in Korean.

I have asked five different Korean Nazarene pastors in Southern California about this matter of probationary members. Their mutual response was: "We accept them but need to grow them in faith," and, "If Koreans know we will put them under the probationary category, no one would join us." I found that no Korean pastors use a direct translation of the term, neither in Southern California nor in Oklahoma, where I worked for eight years.

When the Church of the Nazarene began from her American roots, this was a unique church among American Christians. But Korean members are not coming from nominal Christianity or though the waves of a great holiness movement. These people are coming in families who turned away from their long held traditional gods. In Korean thinking a persons' relation to a group is either in or out, so if a Korean in the process of conversion is received as a "probational member," that person will tend to feel alienated as an outsider to the group. This will cause the person to feel uncomfortable and shameful, and may result in their dropping out of the church fellowship. Korean Nazarene pastors tend to circumvent this system altogether, due to its inappropriateness to their culture.

Considering the cooperative mentality and the tendency of conversion as a process, I propose that the Korean church would benefit by using the term "preparatory member" and focus on raising the person in a holy life.

Sunday School. With respect to the education of children, it is natural for the American churches to expect that because Korean children are growing up in America, they should attend the American children's Sunday school. But like their parents, Korean children are culturally and behaviorally different from their American counterparts and, like my own nephews and nieces, express to their parents that they don't want to go. The non-attendance by Korean children to local or district programs can be recognized as evidence of the cultural distance and alienation that Koreans feel. Therefore, I recommend that Korean Nazarene leaders act on forming their own activities in the Korean language at both the local and the district level.

Worship Format. A first-generation church holds services in the Korean language and worships in the Korean way. However, a bilingual service should be held for the 1.5-generation church, while the second-generation church and children's church should be conducted in English. Korean leaders must contextualize to these graded levels, while keeping the reality of influences of both cultures in mind.

The stereotypical Korean Sunday morning worship, which is very formal, translated in English is not what I recommend. Neither is an entirely American contemporary worship fully appropriate. Contextualization of the worship format needs to be open ended to allow for a suitable re-contextualization for the second generation.

Budget. Presently there are three organized and four mission-type Churches of the Nazarene in Southern California. The rule of thumb is that when a mission type Korean congregation uses an American church facility, they pay 10 percent of their offerings to the American local church and 10 percent to the district. But when the Korean congregation reaches the status of being an organized church, they must add to these payments the general budget.

In a meeting with three Southern California Korean pastors, it was pointed out that the burden of payment was heavy to a weak and struggling ethnic church, and that one result was that people hesitated joining the church. They said, "If the Korean churches were receiving any benefit from the general or district levels, they would not think this way." But the linguistic and cultural differences prevent the Koreans from receiving the benefits that are offered. "Being a small and unknown denominational church, we must invest funds more for evangelistic activities and for local church growth," said Joo and Kim in an interview of Oct. 25, 1991.

I propose a recommendation that young Korean churches be temporarily relieved of paying general budgets and focus on the growth of their local churches until they are sizable enough to pay general budgets. If this helps the church to grow, it would benefit the general church in the long run.

Use of the American Church Facilities. Policies regarding the actual use of the building and church facilities pose a constant challenge for the Korean immigrant church. Since the average American church doesn't have midnight prayer meetings, dawn prayer meetings, or Friday night prayer meetings, it is difficult for them to allow their building to be used so frequently. Because of this, tension arises and Koreans lose out on something that is very important to them.

In some cases the Korean church is given use of the building for three hours on Sunday and one hour Friday night. Even the signboard can be a problem. Some Korean churches were not allowed to display their church signboard, an understandably important matter. Korean pastor Kang expressed the importance of the problem, "If a church wants to grow, the building needs to be used as frequently as possible and sign board is a must" (Oct. 25, 1991).

It is normal for the host Anglo-American congregation to feel protective about their facilities when it comes to noise and even foreign smells. These may seem to be administrative details, but such things are important to the self-expression of both American and Korean congregations. To withhold use of these facilities sends a negative message about how seriously the local church takes mission to be. I sometimes get the feeling that the Korean mission congregations are a burden and a bother to sponsoring churches. But in open dialogue and through greater sensitivity to the cultural differences on both sides, there is nothing that cannot be worked out satisfactorily.

Housing a Korean Church in its Own Facility. Some Korean churches of the Nazarene maintain their own facilities, separate from an American church. In my experience two of these are Oklahoma Korean Church of the Nazarene in Oklahoma City and Anaheim Korean Church of the Nazarene in Anaheim, CA. With free use of the building, and no cultural conflicts with the host congregation, every church activity is calculated to meet the needs of the people. Being unhindered by cultural differences, and having a sense of ownership for the property, these churches seem to do better than others. Naturally having one's own facilities is conducive to growth.

When Cho Moon Kyung planted a congregation, the Southern California District generously gave him decent worship facilities and a parsonage. His church has become the largest Korean Church of the Nazarene in Southern California, having over 200. They had their own prayer meetings, Bible studies and other activities without restriction.

The Oklahoma Korean Church of the Nazarene in Oklahoma City, where Yoon Kyu Chun pastored, had separate housing. The church has grown to 150 members out of a Korean population of approximately 1,000. The freedom and ownership of facilities have been important to them. People feel at home when they come to their own facility. Therefore, most Korean pastors and churches dream of having their own building.

Church Life. Koreans' Christian life is fundamentally the same as Americans', but their forms are sometimes different. Fellowship meals after Sunday worship, daily dawn prayer meetings, Friday midnight prayer meetings, and occasional all night vigils are very important to the normal functioning of Korean church life. For the church to grow, they must be able to do these activities.

Korean language school for the children on Saturday is an important part of nearly every church, as parents wish to preserve their language and culture among the youth. Doing all these activities requires a great deal of facility use. Both American and Korean pastors must recognize this and be prepared to cooperate for the sake of the church's growth.

Putting the Trajectory into Action. With reference to the trajectory principle, the "contents" are contextualized theology and ecclesiology. The container in which they are presented is the church. If the "trajectory," the necessary degree of contextualization, is properly analyzed by local, district, and general leaders, and the "thrust," the energy and resources required to contextualize, is given, I believe we will see a new movement of growth among our Korean churches. After some time, perhaps two decades, we will need further re-contextualization for the second-generation Korean Church.

IN PARTING

I am aware that while the first-generation Korean Church of the Nazarene needs contextualization for communicating the Christian truth in their cultural and linguistic context, it is also urgent that we re-contextualize for the 1.5 and second generations. As I previously mentioned, the 1.5 generation is bilingual and bicultural, and they struggle with their transitional identity. They feel separation from their own roots, and cultural identity. They receive American education under American teachers, yet their worldview and value systems are closer to those of the Korean families. Therefore, they struggle and conflict with Korean culture. Yet in their college years they become increasingly positive about their identity as Korean-Americans.

We have looked rather extensively into a variety of issues that tend to divide the Korean Church from the American Church of the Nazarene. Our attention has been given to the particular histories of the two streams from the cultural, theological, and ecclesiological points of view. The problem we stated at the outset raised the point that due to the American identity of the Nazarene Church, in contrast to the cultural baggage carried to America by immigrant Koreans, there is conflict between the two groups, and there are reasons why adjustments between the two groups have been so difficult.

It has been a most enlightening process to appreciate the hard facts of two very different worlds attempting to accomplish the Lord's work together "under one roof" so to speak. In conclusion, it might be mentioned that certain modifications in the "Nazarene way" of approaching worship and governing the church have been made for the Nazarene churches in Korea. To some extent these represent models for what is needed to bring about beneficial changes that might take place in the U.S.A. The old proverb may be revalidated, "When in America become acculturated enough to do as the Americans do."

Therefore, in referring once more to what I have called the trajectory principle: A trajectory is always open-ended and flexible. At any point where it hits its target, one must be ready to put it back into motion aiming it at a new context created as a culture goes through changes.

May God give us the love and patience to work together and the commitment to fulfill the tasks he has given.

NOTES

Chapter 2 - The Rise of the Church of the Nazarene U.S.A.

1. Being in a West coast context, Bresee's idea of the life of holiness centered less on outward appearances and more on internal commitments. Had his approach been more widely accepted, the church might have been more amenable to Korean contextualization.

Chapter 3 - Contextualization

1. For further reading on this subject see Robert Schreiter, Constructing Local Theologies. New York: Orbis Books, 1985, p.21.

2. All biblical references are taken from the New International Version.

3. For further reading on these models see Schreiter (1985:6–16), Dean Gilliland, ed. (1989:313–317), and Stephen Bevans (1985:185–200).

Chapter 4 - Korean Worldview (A): Shamanism

1. The original Korean pronunciation is "Hanulnim" or "Hanunim." Every non-Christian knows "Hanunim" as the only and absolute God, who rules over heaven and earth, and who knows the human heart. Thus this concept prepared the way for "Hananim" to be understood and accepted as the Christian God.

2. These *kuts* are performed by the shamen immediately after funeral services are held to keep the family from dead spirits' hovering and harm.

3. Mountains are considered sacred and separated from the world, which is why Buddhist temples were generally built in the mountains, and why modern Christian prayer houses are built in the mountains.

4. Since people experience healing by *kut*, it is natural for them to believe, and even expect, that God will likewise heal.

5. A *mudang* blesses the family with sacrifices and by *kut*. When people become Christian, they also expect God's blessings and habitually seek after them in much the same way.

Chapter 5 - Korean Worldview (B): Buddhism, Confucianism and Christianity

1. For further reading see Joong Young Lee 1982:13–18

2. The "middle zone" is between the sphere of the natural on the one hand and the transcendent, other-worldly, supernatural on the other. It is of this world, while at the same time being supernatural.

Chapter 6 - Comparison of Korean and American Worldview Themes

1. Twelve animals symbolize time as being cyclical. Therefore, Koreans do not view time as being lost, gained, saved, or wasted.

2. The closest western concept to *palcha* might be that of one's fate or destiny. *Palcha* originates in *saju*: one's year, month, day, and hour of birth. It is a thoroughly pervasive concept and is used to explain any and all things in life, both good and bad.

3. When the wedding partner is decided, the couple exchanges verification of their *saju*.

Chapter 7 - The Korean Church of the Nazarene in the U.S.A.

1. The steps of the revitalization process are 1. Old steady state; 2. Increased individual stress; 3. Cultural distortion; 4. Revitalization; 5. New steady state.

2. The concept of the "mental map" originates with Charles Kraft and relates to the concept of worldview and worldview change. The basic stages of this concept are 1. what one is taught or believes is true; 2. what one subsequently experiences; 3. what one actually reflects on and affirms or changes; 4. the resulting mental paradigm or "map" one adheres to.

3. The consanguineous group is very common in Korea due to Korea's monolithic and monocultural nature. Bloodline is very important and plays a significant role in social and political relations.

4. Many churches have Saturday Korean school, where they teach Korean language and culture to second-generation children. During summer vacations some churches also organize student trips to Korea.

Chapter 8 - Contextualization and Conclusion

1. See Kraft 1979:294–302 where he says, "A relevant Gospel message is to be understood as being relevant to the hearer in their context."

2. These terms were first used by Ralph Winter in 1974 and broke open a whole new way of thinking about cross-cultural missions. For further information on this see Winter's observations quoted in McGavran (1980:63–69).

3. While the concepts of fate and predestination have similarities, fate is mechanistic, impersonal and unconcerned with a person's well-being. Predestination on the other hand is under the sovereignty of God and is personal and entirely concerned with a person's well-being. This theological reformulation is not only contextually effective, but also very attractive to those undergoing conversion.

4. *Moksa* means "shepherding teacher." Unless a pastor is ordained, people will not refer to him as moksa, even if he is pastoring a church.

REFERENCES CITED

Allmen, Daniel von
    1975a   "The Birth of Theology." *International Review of Mission* 64 (253): 37–52.

Barclay, William
    1964   *Turning to God: A Study of Conversion in the Book of Acts and Today.* Grand Rapids, MI: Baker Book House.

Barth, Christopher
    1967   "Notes on 'Return' in the Old Testament." *The Ecumenical Review* 19 (3): 310–312.

Bellah, Robert N., et. al.
    1985   *Habits of the Heart: Individualism and Commitment in American Life.* New York, NY: Harper & Row.

Bercovitch, Scavan
    1975   *Puritan Origins of American Self.* New Haven, CT: Yale University Press.

Berger, Peter, Brigitte Berger, and Hansfried Kellner
    1967   *The Sacred Canopy.* Garden City, NY: Doubleday.

    1974   *The Homeless Mind.* New York, NY: Vintage Books.

Bevans, Stephen
    1985   "Models of Contextual Theology." *Missiology* 13 (2): 185–202.

Blair, William Newton
    1957   *Gold in Korea*, 3rd edition. New York, NY: Central Distributing Department of the Presbyterian Church in the U.S.A.

Brown, Colin, ed.
    1975   *The New International Dictionary of New Testament Theology.* Vol. 1. Grand Rapids, MI: Zondervan.

Brown, Robert Macaffee
    1977   "The Rootedness of All Theology: Context Affects Content." *Christianity in Crisis* 37 (July): 170–174.

Buswell, J. Oliver III
    1978   "Contextualization: Theory, Tradition and Method." In *Theology and Mission.* David J. Hesselgrave, ed. Grand Rapids, MI: Baker Book House.

Cadogan, Leon
    1962   *Aporte a la etnografia los guarani del Amabai.* Alto Ypane. RASP Vol. 10, 43–91.

Chang, Yunsik
    1982   "Shamanism as Folk Existentialism." In *Religions in Korea: Beliefs and Cultural Values.* E.H. Phillips and Eui Young Yu, eds. Los Angeles, CA: Center for Korean-American and Korean Studies, California State University.

Chung, Chai-Sik
    1982   "Confucian Tradition and Values: Implications for and Conflict in Modern Korea." *In Religion in Korea: Beliefs and Cultural Values.* E.H. Phillips and Eui-Young Yu, eds. Los Angeles, CA: Center for Korean-American and Korean Studies, California State University.

Clark, Allen D.
    1971   *A History of the Korean Church.* Seoul: The Christian Literature Society of Korea (1st edition, 1930).

Clark, Charles A.
  1929   *Religions of Old Korea.* Seoul: The Christian
          Literature Society of Korea.

Coe, Shoki, and Aharon Sapsezian
  1972   *Ministry in Context: The Third Mandate Programme
          of the Theological Education Fund.* London:
          Theological Education Fund, WCC.

Cole, Stewart G. and Mildred Wiese Cole
  1954   *Minorities and the American Promise.* New Haven,
          CT: Yale University Press.

Commager, Henry Steele
  1950   *The American Mind: An Interpretation of American
          Thought and Character Since the 1880's.* New
          Haven, CT: Yale University Press.

Conn, Harvie
  1984   *Eternal Word and Changing World.* Grand Rapids,
          MI: Zondervan.

Crèvecoeur, Hector St. John De
  1981   *Letters from an American Farmer.* New York, NY:
          Penguin Books (1st edition 1782).

DeGrazia, Sebastian
  1971   "Time and Work." *In The Future of Time, Man's
          Temporal Environment.* Henri Yaker, et al., eds.
          Garden City, NY: Anchor.

Dix, Griffin
  1982   "Economic, Social, and Cultural Effects of the
          Geomancy of House Sites." In *Religions in Korea:
          Beliefs and Cultural Values.* Eui Y. Yu and E. H.
          Phillips, eds. Los Angeles, CA: Center for Korean-
          American and Korean Studies, California State
          University.

Durkheim, Emile
 1947   *The Elementary Forms of Religious Life*. Translated
         by Joseph W. Swain. New York, NY: The Free Press
         (1st edition 1912).

Eliade, Mircea
 1959   *The Sacred and the Profane: The Nature of Religion*.
         New York, NY: Harcourt, Brace and Company.

 1964   *Shamanism: Archaic Techniques of Ecstasy*.
         Translated from French by Willard R. Trask.
         Kingsport, TN: Pantheon Books.

Fisher, James E.
 1970   *Democracy and Mission Education in Korea*. New
         York, NY: Teachers College, Columbia University
         Press.

Foster, George
 1973   *Traditional Culture and the Impact of Technological
         Change*. New York, NY: Harper & Row (1st edition
         1962).

Gabriel, Ralph Henry
 1956   *The Course of American Democratic Thought*. New
         York, NY: The Ronald Press Company.

Gilliland, Dean S.
 1983   "Contextual Theology as Incarnational Mission." In
         *The Word Among Us: Contextualizing Theology for
         Mission Today*. Dean S. Gilliland, ed. Dallas, TX:
         Word.

Girvin, Ernest Alexander
 1916   *Phineas F. Bresee: A Prince in Israel*, a Biography.
         Kansas City, MO: Pentecostal Nazarene Publishing
         House.

Gordon, Milton
  1964   *Assimilation in American Life: The Role of Race,
            Religion, and National Origins*. New York, NY:
            Oxford University Press.

"Guidelines for Multi-Congregational Ministries of the L.A.
District"
  c.1989   Pasadena, CA: L.A. District Church of the Nazarene.

Guillermoz, Alexandre
  1973   "The Religious Spirit of the Korean People." *Korea
            Journal*. 12 (5): 12–18.

Haleblian, Krikor
  1982   "Contextualization and French Structuralism: A
            Method to Delineate the Deep Structures of the
            Gospel" Ph.D. Dissertation, Pasadena, CA: Fuller
            Theological Seminary.

Hall, Edward T.
  1981a   *Beyond Culture*. Garden City, NY: Anchor Books
            (1st edition, Doubleday, 1976).

  1981b   *The Silent Language*. Garden City, NY: Anchor
            Books (1st edition, Doubleday, 1959).

Hearn, Soo-Goon
  1989   Personal interview. Los Angeles, CA, January 20.

Heikkinen, J.W.
  1968   "Notes on 'Epistrepho' and 'Metanoeo.'" *The
            Ecumenical Review* 19 (3): 313–316.

Hesselgrave, David and Edward Rommen
  1989   *Contextualization: Meanings and Models*. Grand
            Rapids, MI: Baker Book House.

Hiebert, Paul
    1982   "The Flaw of the Excluded Middle." In *Missiology: And International Review* 10:35–47.

    1985   *Anthropological Insights for Missionaries*. Grand Rapids, MI: Baker Book House.

    1987   Class Syllabus, MR 520, "Phenomenology and Institutions of Folk Religions." Pasadena, CA: Fuller Theological Seminary, School of World Mission.

Hohensee, Donald Wilhelm
    1980   "Rundi Worldview and Contextualization of the Gospel: A Study in Theologizing in Terms of Worldview Themes." D.Miss. Dissertation, Pasadena, CA: Fuller Theological Seminary.

Hoebel, Adams
    1972   *Anthropology: A Study of Man,* 4th edition. New York, NY: McGraw-Hill.

Hulbert, Holmer
    1969   *The Passing of Old Korea*. Seoul: Yonsei University Press.

Im, Tong-Gwon
    1973   "Pyolsin Exorcism of Ulsan (I)." *Korea Journal* 13 (11): 4–9.

Inch, Morris
    1982   *Doing Theology Across Cultures*. Grand Rapids, MI: Baker Book House.

Kang, Young Seok
    1991   Personal interview. Los Angeles, CA, October 25.

Kasdorf, Hans
    1980   *Christian Conversion in Context*. Scottdale, PA: Herald Press.

Kearney, Michael
1984   *World View*. Novato, CA: Chandler & Sharp.

Keesing, R.M. and F.M. Keesing.
1971   *New Perspective in Cultural Anthropology*. New York: Holt, Rinehart and Winston.

Kennedy, Ruby Jo Reeves
1944   "Single or Triple melting Pot? Intermarriage trends in New Haven, 1870–1940." *Journal of Sociology* 49:331.

Kietzman, Dale W.
1974   "Conversion and Culture Change." In *Readings in Missionary Anthropology*. William Smalley, ed. Pp. 124–131. Pasadena: William Carey Library.

Kim, Chan Hie
1982   "Christianity and Modernization of Korea." In *Religions in Korea: Beliefs and Cultural Values*. E.H. Phillips and Eui Young Yu, eds. Los Angeles, CA: Center for Korean-American and Korean Studies, California State University.

Kim, Duk-Hwang
1988   *A History of Religions in Korea*. Seoul: Daeji Moonhwa-Sa.

Kim, Hei Chu
1982   "Confucianism and Social Integration in Yi Dynasty Korea." In *Religions in Korea: Beliefs and Cultural Values*. E.H. Phillips and Eui Young Yu, eds. Los Angeles, CA: Center for Korean-American and Korean Studies, California State University.

Kim, Jong Il
1985   "Mukyo and Its Implications to the Christian Church in Korea." Ph.D. Dissertation, Pasadena, CA: Fuller Theological Seminary.

Kim, Tae-Gon
    1972   "Components of Korean Shamanism." *Korean Journal* 12 (12): 17–25. Seoul: UNESCO.

    1978   "Shamanism in the Seoul Area." *Korea Journal* 18 (6). Seoul: UNESCO.

Kinslaw, J. Ross
    1978   "Mission and Context: The Current Debate About Contextualization." *Evangelical Mission Quarterly* 14 (1): 23–30.

Ko, Young Bok
    1978   "Principle-Subordinate Relationship." Korea Journal 18 (10). Seoul: UNESCO.

Koyama, Koske
    1974   *Waterbuffalo Theology*. Maryknoll, NY: Orbis Books.

Kraft, Charles
    1979   *Christianity in Culture: A Study in Dynamic Biblical Theologizing in Cross-Cultural Perspective*. Maryknoll, NY: Orbis Books.

    1982   Class syllabus, MB 520, "Anthropology," Pasadena, CA. Fuller Theological Seminary, School of World Mission.

    1989   "Contextualizing Communication." *In The Word Among Us*. Dean Gilliland, ed. Dallas, TX: Word Publishing.

Latourette, Kenneth Scott
    1940   "Indigenous Christianity in the Light of History." *International Review of Missions* 29:429–431.

1975 *A History of Christianity*. Vol. II: *Reformation to the Present*, Rev. edition. New York, NY: Harper & Row.

Leach, E.R.
1966 *Rethinking Anthropology*. New York: Humanitics.

Lee, Grant S.
1976 "The Confucian Weltanshauung: An Extension of Filial Axis." *Korea Journal* 16 (4). Seoul: UNESCO.

Lee, Jung Young
1982 "The Book of Change and Korean Thought." In *Religions in Korea: Beliefs and Cultural Values*. E.H. Phillips and Eui Young Yu, eds. Los Angeles, CA: Center for Korean-American and Korean Studies, California State University.

Lee, Kwang Rin
1976a "Positive Progressive Views on Protestantism I." *Korea Journal* 16 (2). Seoul: UNESCO.

1976b "Positive Progressive Views on Protestantism II." *Korea Journal* 16 (3). Seoul: UNESCO.

Lee, Man Gap
1982 *Sociology and Social Change in Korea*. Seoul: National University.

Luzbetak, Louis, J.
1970 *The Church and Cultures*. Pasadena, CA: William Carey Library.

1981 "Signs of Progress in Contextual Methodology." *Uerluem* 22: 39–57.

MacCulloch, John Arnott
    1958   "Shamanism." In *Encyclopedia of Religion and Ethics*. Vol. 2. James Hastings, ed. New York, NY: Charles Scribner's Sons.

Machen, Gresham
    1947   *The Origin of Paul's Religion*. Grand Rapids, MO: Eerdmans.

Manual of the Church of the Nazarene
    1911   Publishing House of the Pentecostal Church of the Nazarene, General Assembly.

    1939   Kansas City, MO: Nazarene Publishing House.

    1989   Kansas City, MO: Beacon Hill.

McGavran, Donald
    1980   *Understanding Church Growth*, Rev. edition. Grand Rapids, MI: Eerdmans.

Metraux, Alfred
    1928   "The Guarani." *The South American Indian* 31: 69–94.

Min, Kyung Bae
    1982   *A History of the Korean Church*. Seoul: Christian Literature Society of Korea.

Moon, Sang-hi
    1974   "A Historical Survey of Korean religion." *Korea Journal* 14 (5) Seoul: Si-sa-Yong-o-sa.

Morey-Gaines, Ann-Janine
    1979   *Apples and Ashes: Culture, Metaphor, and Morality in the American Dream*. American Academy of Religion Academy Series, no. 38. Chico, CA: Scholars Press.

Mumford, Lewis
    1963   *Technics and Civilization*. New York, NY: Harcourt (1st edition 1934).

Newbigin, Leslie
    1986   *Foolishness to the Greeks*. Grand Rapids, MI: Eerdmans.

Nicholls, Bruce
    1979   *Contextualization: A Technology of Gospel and Culture*. Downers Grove, IL: InterVarsity Press.

Nida, Eugene A.
    1981   *Customs and Cultures*. Pasadena, CA: William Carey Library.

Orr, J. Edwin
    1975a   *The Flaming Tongue*. Chicago, IL: Moody Press.

    1975b   *Evangelical Awakenings in Eastern Asia*. Minneapolis, MN: Bethany Fellowship, Inc.

    1981   "The Restudy of Revival and Revivalism." Pasadena, CA: Privately published.

Padilla, C. Rene
    1983   "Biblical Foundations: A Latin American Study." *Evangelical Review of Theology* 7 (1).

Palmer, Spencer
    1967   *Korea and Christianity: The Problem of Identification with Tradition*. Royal Asiatic Society Korea Branch Monograph Series, No. 2. Seoul: Hollym Corp.

Park, Chong-hong
    1975   *The History of Korean Thought*. Seoul: Sumon-dang.

Park, Robert E.
    1930   "Assimilation." In *Encyclopedia of Social Science*.
              Vol. 2. New York, NY: Macmillan Co.

Park, Sung-Bae
    1982   "The Impact of Buddhism on the Axiological System
              Underlying Korean Culture." In *Religions in Korea:
              Beliefs and Cultural Values*. Eui Y. Yu and E. H.
              Phillips, eds. Los Angeles, CA: Center for Korean-
              American and Korean Studies, California State
              University.

Parshall, Phil
    1980   *New Paths in Muslim Evangelism*. Grand Rapids, MI:
              Baker Book House.

Peters, John L.
    1956   *Christian Perfection and American Methodism*.
              Nashville, TN: Abingdon Press.

Piaget, Jean
    1969   *The Child's Conception of Physical Causality.*
              Totowa, NJ: Littlefield, Adams (1st edition 1930).

Poitras, Edward W.
    1977   "The Idea of Self in the Korean Mind." *Korea
              Journal* 17 (12): 14–16. Seoul: UNESCO.

Polman, A.D.R.
    1975   "The Confession in Crisis." In *International
              Reformed Bulletin* 60 (25).

Price, David John
    1979   "The Protestant Understanding of Conversion and
              Implications for Missionary Obedience." Ph.D.
              Dissertation, Pasadena, CA: Fuller Theological
              Seminary.

Purkeiser, W.T., Richard S. Taylor and Willard H. Taylor
    1977   *God, Man and Salvation*. Kansas City, MO: Beacon
            Hill Press.

Redfield, Robert
    1953   *The Primitive World View and Its Transformation*.
            New York, NY: Cornell University Press.

Redfield, Robert, Ralph Linton and Melville J. Herskovits
    1936   "Memorandum for the Study of Acculturation."
            American Anthropologist 38 (1): 149.

Redford, M.E.
    1948   *The Rise of the Church of the Nazarene*. Kansas City,
            MO: Nazarene Publishing House.

Richardson, Don
    1974   *Peace Child.* Glendale, CA: Gospel Light.

Ryu, Tong Shik
    1981   "The World of Gut." *Korea Journal* 13 (8). Seoul:
            UNESCO

"The Seoul Declaration"
    1983   *Evangelical Review of Theology* 7 (1): 8–12.

Shearer, Roy E.
    1966   *Wild Fire: Church Growth in Korea*. Grand Rapids,
            MI: Eerdmans.

Shreiter, Robert J.
    1977   *Constructing Local Theologies*. Chicago, IL: Catholic
            Theological Union, unpublished manuscript.

    1985   *Constructing Local Theologies*. Maryknoll, NY:
            Orbis Books.

Smith, Timothy
1962   *Called Unto Holiness: The Story of the Nazarene Formative Years*. Kansas City, MO: Nazarene Publishing House.

Stewart, George R.
1954   *American Ways of Life*. New York: Doubleday and Co.

Synan, Vinson
1971   *The Holiness Pentecostal Movement in the United States*. Grand Rapids, MI: Eerdmans.

Taber, Charles
1979   "What's New About Contextualization." In *The Missiological Agenda from Charles R. Taber*. Robert T. Coote, ed. Abington, PA: Partnership in Mission.

Tippet, Alan
1973   *Verdict Theology in Mission Theory*. Pasadena, CA: William Carey Library.

Underwood, Horace G.
1908   *The Call of Korea*. New York, NY: Revell.

Von Rad, Gerhard
1962   *Old Testament Theology*. Vol. 1. New York, NY: Harper & Row.

Wagner, C. Peter
1979   *Our Kind of People*. Atlanta, GA: John Knox Press.

1983   Class Syllabus, MC 500, "Church Growth and World Evangelism." Pasadena, CA: Fuller Theological Seminary, School of World Mission.

1985   Plenary address to the National Convocation on Evangelizing Ethnic America. Houston, TX, April.

Wallace, Anthony F.C.
  1956   "Revitalization Movements." *American Anthropologist* 58:264–281.

  1966   *Religion: An Anthropological View*. New York: Random House.

Wasson, Alfred.
  1934   *Church Growth in Korea: Studies in the World Missions of Christianity*. New York, NY: International Missionary Council.

Weems, Clarence Norwood
  1962   *Hulbert's History Of Korea*. 2 Vol. New York, NY: Hillary House Publishers.

Wesley, John
  1829   *The Works of John Wesley*. Thomas Jackson, ed. Vol. XI. London: John Mason.

Williams, Colin W.
  1960   *John Wesley's Theology Today*. New York, NY: Abingdon Press.

Young, Barbara
  1983   "The Lady Fortunetellers of Korea's Cities: There Is a Mysterious Woman in Your Future." In *Traditional Thoughts and Practices of Korea*. Los Angeles, CA: Center for Korean-American and Korean Studies, California State University.

Yu, Eui-Young, Earl Phillips and Eun Sik Yang
  1982   Koreans in Los Angeles: Prospects and Promises. Los Angeles, CA: Center for Korean-American and Korean Studies, California State University.

www.ingramcontent.com/pod-product-compliance
Lightning Source LLC
Chambersburg PA
CBHW071123280326
41935CB00010B/1098